"Maury Davis embodies transparent, authentic leadership. His courage to share and analyze not his greatest successes (which are many and remarkable) but his mistakes injects us with wisdom that can best be described as a preventive vaccination. This is not a must read—it's a must do!"

—Samuel Rodriguez, Senior Pastor, New Season
Christian Worship Center, Sacramento, California

"All leaders make mistakes; but most leaders are too insecure to open the door and see behind the scenes of success to the sacrifices, mistakes, and lessons that led to their success. Pastor Maury Davis opens the door wide, so you can learn from his mistakes—so you don't have to learn from your own. This book will lead you to learn from his mistakes as well as take a good, introspective look at yourself and your leadership."

—Bobby Gourley, Lead Pastor, Chapel, Florence, Alabama

"I have had the honor and privilege of knowing Pastor Maury Davis on a personal level, and I can truly say he is the real deal. In a day in which it seems every other week we are hearing about another well-known minister being exposed for inappropriate behavior, Pastor Maury's honesty and transparency is truly inspiring. As I reflect on this book, I'm reminded of the words of the apostle Paul: "For though you might have ten thousand instructors in Christ, yet you do not have many fathers; for in Christ Jesus I have begotten you through the gospel."

—Bobby Davis, Life Church, Cookeville, Tennessee

"If you look up the word 'Encourager' in the dictionary, you'll find next to it the name Maury Davis. When Pastor Maury speaks, you can be sure you're going to hear timeless wisdom, genuine love, priceless encouragement, and courageous leadership. If you're like me, and could use some of those things, you'll most certainly find them in the pages of this book!"

—Eric Petree, Senior Pastor, CityGate
Church, Cincinnati, Ohio

"As leaders, we can easily fall into the trap of believing that nobody else is as resourceful, intelligent, efficient, or competent as we are. After all, if they were, wouldn't they be the leader? In Maury Davis's book, *Hindsight 20/20*, he recounts some of the common mistakes he made over a lifetime of leading people. These mistakes were not unique to him; in fact, many leaders are on the same frustrated journey on which Maury found himself. As a close friend, I've watched Maury's journey take a pivotal turn as his heart transformed over the years. As Maury struggled to be the strongest leader he could be, he found himself more exasperated than ever. Yet his greatest achievement as a leader was admitting his mistakes and allowing his mind to be renewed to his new discoveries. This book will empower you to make that same journey. Your mistakes can become stepping stones to great successes."

—Ben Dailey, Lead Pastor, Calvary Church, Irving, Texas

"Certain growth can only occur when we take the time to stop and reflect on the mistakes we've made and the lessons we've learned. In *Hindsight 20/20*, our friend, Maury Davis, challenges leaders not to rely on momentum, but to consistently evaluate their methods and motives so that they'll multiply their effectiveness."

—John & Lisa Bevere, Best-Selling Authors and
Ministers, Co-founders of Messenger International

"This is Maury's 'book of a lifetime.' It is raw, vulnerable, real, and very personal. Tears filled my eyes as I turned the pages. Every pastor and leader should read this book!"

—Pastor Rod Loy, First Assembly
North Little Rock, Arkansas

"It was most refreshing reading this amazing literary work of Maury Davis. His naked transparency and willingness to bear his soul to help direct leaders around the pitfalls that the Holy Spirit rescued him from is amazing. It is informative, inspirational, impactful, and instructional, which sets it apart as a must-read for every aggressive leader. When reading it, you hear the therapeutic cry of a loving servant of God who, by the grace of God, is willing to share his past leadership weaknesses to help make the reader a stronger leader. I highly recommend this book to all leaders in business or ministry who desire to please God, lift others, and become more productive in pursuing their life's purpose. Truly an amazing read!"

—Dr. I. V. Hilliard

"I have known Maury Davis for many years now, and not only has his life's journey inspired me, but his honesty has challenged me. In his book, *Hindsight 20/20*, he unlocks his life with 'gut-wrenching' candor, revealing the pitfalls of leadership; yet he leaves us with core values that not only sustain one's personal walk, but position them to be used by God. I know this book will inspire and challenge you!"

—Rusty Nelson, Senior Pastor, Rock Family
Worship Center, Huntsville, Alabama

"Introspection is the tool of the wise and the toy of the fool. Maury Davis's *Hindsight 20/20* provides the leader with a wealth of vulnerable yet valuable lessons that will dynamically engage the leader's life and ministry, regardless of the scale and scope of his or her assignment. The honesty of the book forces the leader to look scrupulously at the driving paradigms and practices that frame his or her current reality. As the author opens up, it evokes the same response from the leader. *Hindsight 20/20* will revolutionize the leader's thinking, and repair and prepare his or her praxis for the next season of success by drawing wisdom from the well of contemplative success."

—Dr. Chris Foster, Cathedral of
Praise, Memphis, Tennessee

I have had the privilege of knowing Maury Davis for nearly thirty years now, and I have watched him grow as a leader and as a pastor who has done some incredible things for God's Kingdom. I engaged him as a coach about two years ago to help me and my son through a succession plan at our church and have gleaned a wealth of knowledge and wisdom from him in the process. In this book Maury bears his soul and becomes truly transparent as he looks back over his ministry and sees the mistakes and failures he went through. I encourage you to open your heart and read his story and perhaps you and I can avoid some of the mistakes that Maury made which is the purpose of this book. I believe I know his heart, that he wants to make us better leaders who avoid the pitfalls and the pain that leaders go through in the leadership journey."

—David Vistine, Senior Pastor, Las Cruces First Assembly of God

"So many books only tell you what the author did right. In his book, *Hindsight 20/20*, Maury is refreshingly transparent and helps guide the reader through mistakes all of us have made at some point. He shows us what it takes to move past the failures and do it right. You can learn from your own mistakes, or you can learn from the mistakes of others. Thank you, Maury, for having the courage to not only admit but to share some of the mistakes you've made along the way, so that we can all learn from them."

—Dr. Dave Martin, Lead Pastor, Motor City Church, Detroit, Michigan

Scripture taken from the NEW AMERICAN STANDARD BIBLE®, Copyright © 1960, 1962, 1963, 1968, 1971, 1972, 1973, 1975, 1977, 1995 by The Lockman Foundation. Used by permission.

Cover Design by Joe DeLeon
Cover Image by Sergey Nivens

ISBN: 978-1-950718-89-4   1 2 3 4 5 6 7 8 9 10

Printed in the United States of America

HINDSIGHT

20/20

MAURY

DAVIS

TEN MISTAKES THAT OFFER
CLARITY AND VISION

AVAIL

CONTENTS

Prologue xi

Introduction xiii

1. I Micromanaged Gifted People 23

2. I Stopped Pursuing Formal Education 43

3. I Was Insensitive to People's Feelings 57

4. I Confused "Authentic" with "Unfiltered" 73

5. I Made Bad Staffing Decisions 87

6. I Was Politically Divisive 103

7. I Didn't Listen to Advice 121

8. I Didn't Celebrate Others' Wins 135

9. I Didn't Take Enough Time to Think 151

10. I Stayed Stuck in Old Ideas 167

Epilogue 181

PROLOGUE

My time on earth has been one challenging, exciting, tragic, victorious journey. Life isn't made up of static emotions, events, or experiences; it's an unexpected roller coaster of twists and turns. As I began the process of writing this book and capturing my thoughts, my purpose wasn't to write a book, but to express to some people I deeply admire my acknowledgments of things in my life that may have been hurtful, disempowering, or even unkind. It was a time of confession, but also a time of inspiration to help others learn the art of TRANS-PARENT INTROSPECTION. I believe, in this super-hyped world we live in, it's critical to developing our leadership influence to learn how to deal with internal issues before we tackle the mountains of life.

As I've learned to be transparent, please do not think this book is meant to be self-demeaning or self-condemning. It's an exercise in being a better person, leader, and friend—not to minimize the good things God has done in my life and the victories He has wrought.

No one gets to where I am without significant input from people. I believe in coaching and consulting, and the personal and organizational transformational power that comes from it. Dr. Ron McManus and Dr. Sam Chand, my two consultants, have helped me over the years to not only transform, grow, and transition the church, but they've also helped Maury Davis become a Maury he would never have met. No words express my sentiments or love for both of you.

As you read this book, instead of being shocked, take the time to ask yourself this: Is there a You that God has in mind for You to meet?

INTRODUCTION

In 1990, Gail and I had just finished a revival in Alabama. We drove up I-65 North, and as we crested the hill and saw the Nashville skyline, we both knew Nashville was going to be home. After years of evangelism, we were being led to settle in to pastor a church. I wanted a church plant to start from scratch. God wanted Cornerstone.

In 1991, we were elected to serve as lead pastors of Cornerstone, a small church that had been birthed in people's basements but had grown to around 200. Nothing about Cornerstone was easy, but everything about it was blessed. On our 20-year anniversary, in 2010, the church held approximately 4,000 people in attendance every Sunday morning. We had 20 years of measurable growth in every major category. We had participated in building and raising money to build 2,000 churches in Kenya. Seven churches were planted out of our congregation. Our TV program reached thousands more every Sunday morning. Cornerstone was a model megachurch, exceeding every expectation. We had reached the pinnacle of success in the church world. Change was coming.

After 20 years, the church became stagnant, and I became frustrated. Nothing worked anymore. Every building campaign, roll call, major event, or decision that had excelled in the past felt counterproductive and produced no growth. I began to question my leadership. I was the problem. In two decades, I hadn't changed my thinking, my education, or my relationships. When the lead pastor is stagnant, the church is stagnant. I had introduced no new philosophy; therefore, we didn't possess any cultural sensitivity. God isn't in the stagnant. He doesn't inhabit that which does not change. God is in growth and life. We pray for comfort for things that are dying because there's nothing to be done. Living is about change, and it is uncomfortable and sometimes painful and hard work. There was work to be done in me.

> *"I am a victim of introspection."*
> —Sylvia Plath

THE PROBLEM

For my entire career, I didn't recognize my mistakes; instead, I maximized those of other people. When I did recognize my mistakes, I apologized; but oftentimes, the damage was done. I didn't think through this strategy and concluded it was the best course. It was entirely intuitive, and it worked well for me. I assumed everyone around me knew that I had their best interests at heart—even when I was gruff and demanding. I was passionate for God's purposes, and I assumed my energy, emotion, and tenacity were enough to convince people to trust me.

When I saw that I'd hurt someone—or on the rare occasions someone actually told me I'd hurt them—I rationalized that accomplishing the mission was much more important than some-one's fragile feelings. Like so many leaders out there, I was task-ori-ented, but I lacked emotional intelligence. I favored IQ over EQ. As culture shifted, that was no longer an effective leadership model. It was never a balanced approach, but it was all I knew.

Raised by an abusive stepfather in a broken home, I was marked by my family. Turning to a life of drugs and crime at a young age, I was marked by society. With all this baggage, many people were at least suspicious of me, and some didn't want to have anything to do with me. They couldn't get past my past, and didn't believe I should be able to get past it, either. They saw me as completely, irredeemably worthless. It was only later that I realized my *real* passion, my *real* goal, my *real* drive—to prove these people wrong. I was determined to succeed. I didn't have a goal to hurt people, and I didn't always go about it the right way; but I was absolutely committed to showing people that I'm bigger than my shame and better than my guilt.

SHADOW MOTIVATION

Along the way, I've received some honors. I've opened the United States Congress in prayer, and I've been the Chaplain of the Day of the Tennessee State Legislature for many years. I've met with the Presi-dent and others in the White House. I've built a large church, and I've received plenty of accolades. All of these were honors, but they were more than that: They were ways I could impress people and shout, "I'm worthy!" And, of course, this drive never went on vacation. It affected every relationship and every decision I made as a leader and a pastor.

When I hurt people, Gail often tried to comfort them: "He didn't really mean that. It's not what he meant to say." Quite often, the offense was (or could have been) a very inconsequential thing; but I had a knack for making mountains out of molehills. I might have barked, "Get that done!" when I could have asked in a polite tone, "Would you be sure to get that done by the end of the day?" I was so laser-focused on accomplishing every task completely and immediately that I didn't consider how I affected people. In everything I said and did, I had two purposes. The stated purpose was to honor God and take the gospel to everyone who would listen; but my *shadow purpose* was to prove that I wasn't who people said I was. I often left people emotionally broken and bleeding; and for that, I'm truly sorry.

In our church, I measured success by dollars in the plate and numbers in the seats. When those are the benchmarks, we use people instead of loving them. I cared more about my staff's production than their spiritual lives or development as leaders. John McKenzie was on our staff for eight years in several different roles. He was insightful enough and courageous enough to speak the truth to me. I remember one occasion in which I gave orders like a drill sergeant. Afterwards, John came up to me and asked, "Pastor, do you still love Jesus?" I couldn't decide if I was offended or chastened.

> *"The inertia of the mind urges it to slide down the easy slope of imagination, rather than to climb the steep slope of introspection."*
> —Marcel Proust

TRANSPARENT INTROSPECTION

When I was in the process of retiring from my role as pastor in 2012, I attended a coaching clinic with Sam and Brenda Chand's Dream Releaser Coaching. It had been years since I'd studied in a classroom or a symposium. For decades, I'd spent all my study time doing sermon preparation. It was in that classroom that I began to have "Aha!" moments. Sam provided an assessment of military leadership vs. relational leadership to me. I remember it as clear as day. I had been a dictator, yet organized and methodical. However, just because he told me that my approach was wrong doesn't mean that I saw the full ramifications at that time. You can hear a solution; but until you introspect, you will never own the change and experience the growth.

In the Chands' training, one of the exercises is to identify change points—negative and positive—at each stage of life, and reflect on the impact of those events. This exercise brought me to my knees. I looked intently at the life of the apostle Paul. Before he met Christ, he had been a powerful, if misdirected, leader. He was a one-man wrecking crew, zealous to stamp out the new movement centered around Jesus as Israel's Messiah. He traveled to cities to arrest, imprison, and even execute Christians. When Stephen was stoned to death for standing up and speaking out for Jesus, Paul was there, approving of every rock thrown. As I read Paul's letters, I saw many things that connected his previous zeal to kill with his new passion to save.

In his letter to the Galatians, Paul describes his experience not long after he met Jesus on the road to Damascus. Christians were understandably skeptical of the change he insisted was real. If they believed him, after all, he could turn on them to arrest them. Many of them kept their distance. As they became convinced that the transformation was genuine, they were amazed. Paul wrote the church in Galatia and told them that, after he went to Jerusalem to meet with Peter and James, he traveled to Syria and Cilicia to tell people about Jesus.

> "I was still unknown by sight to the churches of Judea which were in Christ; but only, they kept hearing, 'He who once persecuted us is now preaching the faith which he once tried to destroy.' And they were glorifying God because of me" (Galatians 1:22-24).

That's what I wanted: I wanted people to see the transformation in me so clearly that they glorified God and praised Him for the wonder of His grace shown to someone as unworthy as me.

But I also saw Paul's raw honesty. He wrote to the young pastor Timothy, "It is a trustworthy statement, deserving full acceptance, that Christ Jesus came into the world to save sinners, among whom I am foremost of all" (1 Timothy 1:15). He explained to the believers in Rome that, even as a Christian, he was well aware of the darkness in his heart. He'd been saved from the penalty of sin, he was being saved from the power of sin, and someday, he would be saved from the presence of sin. In the meantime, he lived with a gigantic internal struggle:

For we know that the Law is spiritual, but I am of flesh, sold into bondage to sin. For what I am doing, I do not understand; for I am not practicing what I would like to do, but I am doing the very thing I hate. But if I do the very thing I do not want to do, I agree with the Law, confessing that the Law is good. So now, no longer am I the one doing it, but sin which dwells in me. For I know that nothing good dwells in me, that is, in my flesh; for the willing is present in me, but the doing of the good is not. For the good that I want, I do not do, but I practice the very evil that I do not want. But if I am doing the very thing I do not want, I am no longer the one doing it, but sin which dwells in me (Romans 7:14-20).

Does that sound like the abundant, victorious Christian life? No—it sounds like the reality of the constant struggle to walk with God and to fight our conflicting desires. Paul asks, "Who will set me free from the body of this death?" (Romans 7:24) Then, he presents the answer: "Thanks be to God through Jesus Christ our Lord! So then, on the one hand I myself with my mind am serving the law of God, but on the other, with my flesh the law of sin" (Romans 7:25-26).

In the coaching clinic, I reflected on all of this. I saw Paul as a leader who practiced transparent introspection and who helped others work through their own conflict. I wanted to be like Paul.

Sam and Brenda's process of reflecting on the segments of my life gave me far more insight than I'd ever had. A thousand puzzle pieces fit together. To be honest, many of them hadn't even been on the table; but God used this exercise to help me find them, identify them, and see how these people and events had shaped my life. I'm not sure which comes first—a commitment to honesty or insight—but I'm convinced that they always go together. This was "transparent intro-spection": peeling back the denial, rationalizing, minimizing, and excusing to see what was really there, and how each stage of my life had affected me. I was finally secure enough to be honest about who

I'd been and how I'd affected people. For the first time, I could see why I thought, believed, spoke, and acted the way I did.

THE CHALLENGE

When I became a pastor, I brought my heart for Jesus, but I also brought a truckload of emotional baggage. I've heard it said that "hurt people hurt people," and that's certainly true for me. After the lights came on for me in the Dream Releaser Coaching sessions, I scheduled a meeting at Cornerstone Church and invited all the people who had been on our staff over the years. I asked them to come in so that I could apologize in person. It was a wonderful, healing time. At the end of our meeting together, several of them told me that I needed to put what I'd said into a book. Other pastors may not have taken the same route I've taken (I sure hope not!), but maybe they can identify with one or two of the mistakes I've made so that they can avoid making them.

I'm not pointing any fingers. I can't take the scales off anyone's eyes, but I can share my story—how God took the scales off my eyes. If the Spirit of God confirms and convicts someone that a change is needed in his or her life, that's between him or her and God. All of us have heard and spoken on the need for integrity and transformation, but personal revelation produces a much deeper conviction than mere information. Your personality may be different from mine. It may not suit you to bring together all of your hurt and mistakes into one room to confront them head-on, in a public manner. You will have to find your own confrontation style when the time comes, but you must begin by confronting yourself.

I'm very much aware of the difference between an explanation and an excuse. In this book, I offer insights I've gained that explain why I've acted the way I have. The issue is never the intended results; the issue is always the approach. We'll discuss ways to approach problems in the correct way—the way that produces the results you need *and* develops the people around you. My "deep dive" into my heart has uncovered buried hurts and previously unnamed compulsions, but I'm not hiding behind anything that might excuse my actions. I take full responsibility for each one.

I hope that, through reading about my mistakes, you will identify your own. I pray you'll do the work to find your shadow motivation and learn transparent introspection. I pray you'll move from being stuck to experiencing positive growth. As you read about my blunders, I'll raise the hood on my life so you can see the inner workings of the engine of my soul. Some of it will be funny, but most of it will make you cringe. If you don't look back at yourself and cringe, then you're not growing. That's okay with me—it's who I've been; but, thank God, it's not who I'm becoming.

I MICROMANAGED GIFTED PEOPLE

"Micromanagement is the destroyer of momentum."
—Miles Anthony Smith

Over eight years of incarceration, Pastor J. Don George regularly came to see me. As soon as I was released, he hired me onto his staff at Calvary Church. He said, "I want you to go with me." I wasn't sure what he meant, but I soon found out.

I met Pastor George at his house at 5:45 AM every morning for a six-mile run around Bachman Lake. I watched him dictate letters, I went to the hospital with him to visit the sick, and he invited me to join him at his Rotary Club meetings. I was with him all the time, except for his one-on-one meetings. He even took me on a family vacation, so I could see how he treated his wife and children. I was his personal project; after six months, I was qualified to be the church janitor. He wanted to truly disciple me and make certain that I was ready to begin serving in the church.

Pastor George passed away as this book was being published, but he was a man of immaculate neatness. He was always perfectly dressed, his car was vacuumed, and his desk was neatly arranged. Nothing in his life was out of order—and, if he could help it, nobody else's life was out of order, either. When the church moved to a new facility, he went to every staff member's new office to arrange their bookshelves and hang pictures. He taught me to be more than an observer—he taught me to look for people who could be disciples. I had learned at the military academy that I functioned far better in a structured environment, and Pastor George's world fit me perfectly. Others may kick against structure, but rules are my friends.

I had a number of roles at Calvary. I started as a janitor, but I was more of an observer; then, a personal assistant; an executive assistant for construction projects; and finally, a youth pastor. It was amazing that the parents asked for me—someone who'd been out of prison less than two years—to be the role model and teacher to their kids; but God gave us favor. You can't disqualify God's plan. I was asked to go on TBN and PTL. A local station gave me a slot on Thursday nights before Jimmy Swaggart. Within six weeks, our ratings were equal to his.

In 1991, Gail and I and our four-year-old triplets drove into Nashville, Tennessee, with full hearts and a calling to build a church. God's plan led us to Cornerstone Church, which averaged around 200 and had grown exponentially from meeting in various homes in the community. The excitement was palpable, but the congregation was tired from transition and ready to move forward.

I was determined to instill a passion for excellence. Still, we had a long way to go. The only thing growing in the flowerbeds was a stunning variety of weeds. The sanctuary had brown and white kitchen tile on the floor, black chairs with silver legs, and red steps leading up to a blue platform. The roof trusses and stained glass windows held the only redeeming design value in the place. From the day I arrived, we were so far behind on the mortgage payments that Gail and I had to use the little bit of money we'd made from the sale of our Dallas duplex to keep the bank from foreclosing. Contributions were so sparse that I had to work loading and unloading trucks two nights a week so we'd have enough money to live. We saved enough to pay for paint, so we could make the church at least look a little better.

From the first moment I laid eyes on the church and committed myself to excellence, I was sure it wasn't going to happen unless I made all the decisions and oversaw every detail. The previous pastor hadn't exactly left in a blaze of glory. People were upset with him, and they didn't know me. There was plenty of dissension. They wanted to know who I'd select for the board because they wanted to know which side I'd take in their disputes. Pastor George didn't have these problems because he was a legacy leader. I decided it was time for me to take a stand. I preached a message out of Micah 4:9, in which God told the whiners, "Now, why do you cry out loudly? Is there no king among you, or has your counselor perished, that agony has gripped you like a woman in childbirth?" I told our congregation, "I can't find anywhere in the Scriptures where God appoints a board to run His church. As long as I'm your pastor, I'll make the decisions about the direction of the church." I guess they were tired of bickering, because they gave me a standing ovation. I took this as confirmation that my way was the only way.

As Cornerstone began to grow and we hired a few people for our staff team, I told each one to make a detailed list of things they needed to do each day. I checked their schedule daily. When I examined them, if they weren't doing everything I wanted them to do, I called them in for a reprimand and some redirection. I'd say, "You've been doing this, but I want you to do that. If you do that, our church will grow. Do you understand? Okay, now make this change and get back with me." I had confused Pastor George's discipleship with micromanagement.

> *"Never tell people how to do things. Tell them what to do,*
> *and they will surprise you with their ingenuity."*
> —General George S. Patton

When I was at Calvary, John McKenzie—our junior high pastor— and I had summer camp for 300 at the beach, and I made him put particular kids in specific rooms. When he brought me the list, I made changes. He told me, "Pastor, these four are good friends, and they want to be together … and these four … and these."

I didn't budge. "We need to have two new people in each of those rooms, so they can get to know other kids. And besides, I want to break up the cliques in the youth group." I also asked him to assign kids to each van, and if I didn't like the mix, I changed it. I went over every minute of the schedule—every detail—including meals, acceptable types of bathing suits, the dress code for our adult sponsors, and the spiritual maturity of any of the kids onstage in the band, in skits, or giving testimonies. I told John, "Everything needs to meet my standards." It didn't take John long to realize that my standards were very high and personal to me.

When we got to camp, I made John sit with me in the open area of the hotel, where we could see every door on all three floors. I had him create a system, so every student signed out to go to the beach and signed in when they came back. I told John to write the exact time each student went and came back. On the first day, I told him, "You and I are going to park ourselves right here in the open from 7:00 in the morning until our services at 7:00 every night, and when it's over, we'll be here until midnight. We're not going anywhere."

At midnight on the first day, John looked exhausted. He asked, "Can I go to bed now?"

I didn't miss a beat. "No. We need to be sure nobody sneaks out."

John insisted, "But we need some sleep."

I barked back, "We'll go to sleep when this camp is over! I'm not going to have a conversation with parents to tell them we lost their beloved child!"

I didn't trust John with his responsibilities. I didn't trust the sponsors in the rooms to keep an eye on the kids. And I certainly didn't trust the kids to be responsible. Reasonable caution is one thing … compulsive fear is another. I think John learned some things from me about the importance of giving attention to details, but this lesson came at a tremendous cost to my relationship with John.

*"Someone who needs to control their environment
is someone who is motivated by fear."*
—Tina Gilbertson

Why was I so overbearing? I was terrified of failing, so I micro-managed people at Calvary and then at Cornerstone to keep them from contributing to any failure of any kind. I didn't let anyone fail, but I also didn't let anyone develop extraordinary skills that went beyond my capacity to direct everything they did. I was sure different people had skills I'd never have—such as musical talent—but I was just as sure that I knew far better than they how to run the church. I was wrong.

Pastor George had been my pastor, my mentor, and my example of good and godly leadership. I have a strong view of spiritual authority. I haven't made any significant ministry or life decision since I got out of prison without consulting Pastor George. He has never elbowed his way to exercise authority in my life; I've always invited him to give me his input, because I respected him and I'm convinced God put him over me to guide me. That's still true today. The difference is that back then, I was too involved, too restricting, and too directive with people on my team—without being invited. I tried to follow Pastor George's example, but my efforts didn't come across well. Somehow, his involvement in his staff's roles showed admiration and affirmation; mine convinced people I didn't trust or respect them. It was a tragic leadership flaw on my part.

My deep insecurity drove me to work like a gerbil on a wheel—always frantic and running like crazy. I couldn't relax, so I couldn't let anyone else relax. I didn't trust them to have their own styles of ministry, their own contributions to the leadership of the church, or their unique contribution in all we were doing. I never wrote a sermon during the day my first five years as pastor, because I was busy overseeing people. I went to every department staff meeting, and every event, whether I was leading it or not. I wanted to be sure they didn't deviate one bit from my carefully constructed plans. I didn't just sit and listen. I often interrupted: "No, we're not doing it that way. I want you to do it this way." I didn't trust their brains to figure things out; I only trusted *my* brain.

My sense of identity and security was based on the objective, measurable growth of our church and, as a corollary, the opinion of other pastors. The problem, of course, is that comparison was always sitting on my shoulder, whispering to me that, no matter how much we grew, someone else's church was growing faster ... bigger ... better. As we reached each benchmark of growth, I should have been thrilled—and I was, but only for a day or two. I quickly realized another pastor's church was either close on our heels or ahead of us. I wasn't too thrilled about that!

Thankfully, I've changed, but it took me far too long. Recently, I spoke to a group of pastors in South Africa about how to lead during the time of uncertainty brought about by the COVID pandemic. I explained that we need two traits to lead effectively in times of chaos, using a passage from Hebrews: "Therefore, do not throw away your confidence, which has a great reward. For you have need of endurance, so that when you have done the will of God, you may receive what was promised" (Hebrews 10:35-36). Confidence and endurance.

From the time I was a boy, suffering whippings from my stepfather's switches, I've always had endurance. Most people who saw me when I was a pastor assumed I was supremely confident, but it was a mask I wore to hide my rampant insecurity. I was committed to *image management*, and I was more successful at it than I should have been. My confidence was based on my ability to work hard and control every person and every event … not in the truth that God would work in each person and in each circumstance.

By the way, one of the problems of our day is the prevalence of "helicopter parents" and "tiger moms." Parents who smother their children with attention, instructions, and high expectations mean well, but they often have the same effect on their kids that I had on the people on our staff. Their kids get the powerful message that they're incapable of making their own decisions and too incompetent to do well on their own. As children grow, wise parents gradually loosen the reins and let the kids take more responsibility, realizing they'll make some dumb decisions along the way. Within limits—that's the best way for them to learn; it's the only way for them to develop both confidence and endurance.

I hear moms and dads object, "You don't understand. I know better than my kids how their lives should go!" Maybe, but you don't know better than God. We excuse our insecurity because we insist we're protecting our kids from failure, but it's really an effort to keep their failure from being a reflection of our parenting. Just as I had to learn to entrust my staff members to God and to scale back my hyper-controlling behavior, many parents need to entrust their kids to God and back off a bit from being so involved in every detail of their lives.

*"It doesn't make sense to hire smart people and then tell them
what to do; we hire smart people so they can tell us what to do."*
—Steve Jobs

DELEGATING RESPONSIBILITY

Delegating saves time, empowers staff, and allows the organization to work more efficiently. You can't manage the high-level vision while you're constantly in the trenches trying to do everyone else's job for them. It's impossible. You can tell a manager from a leader by how they delegate. A manager assigns tasks across the board and waits for failure. A leader creates space for failure and allows people to fail correctly. "Failing correctly" was a new concept to me. To fail correctly means to fail early, when the stakes aren't high. It means to prepare for failure and give yourself space to fail early and easy so that, when the consequences are dire and correction is impossible, failure is no longer an option.

I didn't create a space where any failure was acceptable. Therefore, I didn't create a space where *growth* was possible. I didn't trust my people to fail, and I certainly didn't trust them to succeed. As a result, they felt defeated and discouraged and stagnant. I'd created a failure-free zone that I thought would comfort my employees: "Come to Cornerstone, where you cannot fail!" Instead, I stifled them, smothered them, and reduced their achievement by reducing failure. You have to have both.

*"The more rules govern, the less freedom and
a sense of self and fulfillment."*
—Dr. Sam Chand

In 2012, I hired Dr. Sam Chand to serve as a coach and consultant to myself and Cornerstone Church. In his assessment, he identified and clearly laid out my command-and-control style of leadership and what it was doing to my staff. His exact words in the assessment were these:

> People might be wary of Pastor Davis's involvement in a 'problem,' because that usually escalates the situation and creates unnecessary tensions and animosities among the people. The best way to understand is that, if the CEO of a $10 million, 125-staff company got involved in purchasing toner for a copier, what signal would that send to the team? I observed the usage of the word "Rule" repeatedly from a number of the persons I spoke with. That word (the vocabulary) "rule" is symbolic of institutional leadership. That means someone creates the rule and others abide by it. In that culture, people don't rise to the level of leading by principles and becoming thought leaders.

> My staff was scared of my involvement. They could repeat my vision, but they didn't understand it or own it. And I *wanted* the people to be happy. When my leadership didn't make them happy, I was angry and exhausted, and we were stuck in a constant cycle of mutual frustration. I was absolutely influenced by militaristic leaders, from prison to military school to Pastor George. The differences between Military

vs. Civilian leadership principles are significant. Dr. Chand provided me with the following chart:[1]

MILITARY	CIVILIAN
Move quickly	Move slowly
About the end result	About the process
Clear about chain of command	Build a network of chains of command
Team orientation	Individual orientation
Limited bureaucracy	Total bureaucracy
Quick decision making	Feasibility and "what ifs" dominate.
Yes, AND	Yes, BUT
Challenges you to move aggressively in visionary directions with little patience for delays	Have challenges with those they perceive as pushing through their agendas
Little talk—more action	Talk and then some more talk
Trained BEFORE for what they do	Trained AFTER they get the job
Sensitive about the *chain of command*	Concerned about the *chain of events*
Authoritarian (Accomplishing the task is the main issue.)	Librarians ("On what shelf do I put this task? Is it in the P or the S Section?")
Motivated by others and their wishes/commands	Motivated by inner motivation
An order is to be executed	An order is an invitation to debate.
A decision is final.	A decision can always be re-visited by bureaucracy.

---

1 Sam Chand came to Cornerstone in 2012 at my request. I expected him to give me an assessment of our organizational challenges, but instead, he provided a referendum on my leadership. He identified why my leadership was losing traction and holding back the growth of the church. It was a brutal but necessary conversation.

Steve Jobs is one of the most notoriously successful micromanagers of all time. He was known for being harsh with his team but always getting the best out of people. He micromanaged so much that he even worked in an Apple store and designed the glass steps we now see in the brick-and-mortar locations. He couldn't let go of the details. When Jobs returned to join Apple as CEO, he knew he had to change his management style to take his company (and his people) to the next level.

Jobs created a structure in which there was no dictator, no hierarchy of ideas, and no micromanagement. He didn't have to have all the ideas or execute every single plan. Instead, he created an environment where the best idea won, instead of the person with the highest educational credentials or the most personality. His company was based on products. He allowed the best ideas to surface, and then collaborated to make them even better. Collaboration doesn't kill momentum when it has checkpoints to ensure progress.

"Leadership embraces failure of your people when it leads to growth."
—Seth Godin

We can imagine the grief and fear Jesus' followers felt when the Jewish leaders and Romans executed Jesus … and then, their stunned delight when He appeared to them after the resurrection. Forty days later, it was time for Him to go, but His followers still didn't get it. They asked, "Lord, is it at this time You are restoring the kingdom of Israel?" I can imagine Jesus shaking His head at the question; however, He responded by entrusting them with the greatest enterprise the world has ever known: "… [B]ut you will receive power when the Holy Spirit has come upon you; and you shall be My witnesses both in Jerusalem, and in all Judea and Samaria, and even to the remotest part of the earth" (Acts 1:8).

I have to ask myself, "Maury, would you entrust your church to Peter, who was a paragon of inconsistency? Would you entrust the future of your church to some fishermen, a tax collector, a rebel zealot, and a few others with absolutely no credentials … who had shown remarkable lack of insight?" Jesus did. Jesus didn't wait until His disciples did things perfectly before He gave them more responsibility than they ever dreamed they'd shoulder. He saw potential in them when they didn't see it in themselves, and He did the opposite of micromanaging them—He left the scene and left them in charge. He trusted the Holy Spirit to work so powerfully in them and through them that their impact would be an unmistakable sign that the new kingdom had, in fact, come.

I'd read these passages dozens or maybe hundreds of times, but I hadn't seen the obvious leadership principle because I hadn't *wanted* to see it. Loosening my grip felt too uncomfortable, too threatening. It took me 30 years to see this truth and to make some changes in light of it.

I met Dana Lawson when he and his future wife began attending Cornerstone Church. As he and Julia became more involved, their exemplary service put them on my radar. Later, I hired Dana to be our CFO. In many ways, he went far beyond his job description. Because he was so intuitive, he became a person of influence with many staff members. During his time at Cornerstone, he was a difference maker. Take a look at what he has to say about his experience.

AS I SHARE MY THOUGHTS and experiences about working for a "micromanager," I'd like to start by saying that the term itself doesn't indicate that an individual is arrogant or self-centered. In many cases, it's quite the opposite. To me, "micromanager" indicates that the leader cares so much that he or she literally believes success or failure lies solely on his or her ability to know and manage every detail.

In my experience with Maury Davis, I found his style of leadership to be frustrating on one hand, but safe on the other. Maury believed it was critical to the organization that he be involved in every decision. I'm sure it made sense to him, since he came to the organization when it was in bad financial shape and near foreclosure. The money, time, effort, and family sacrifice he invested convinced him that no one could care as much about the organization as he did and, therefore, couldn't do as good of a job leading it. This also became his barometer for how much other people cared about the organization: "How much are they willing to sacrifice for it?"

This type of leadership worked when the church was small; but as it grew, Maury's need to stay involved with every decision quickly stifled the organization's ability to function at a high level. The rest of the people on the team, no matter what positions they held, were always waiting for a decision from Maury.

This type of management style produces a mindset that others can't lead—they can only manage. They can't make decisions—they can only carry them out. While this is frustrating and slows the organization down, it also does something else negative in a staff member's career: I found myself taking comfort in the fact that, if Maury made the decisions, the outcome was "on him." Therefore, in an effort to avoid making mistakes or being seen as failing, I simply had to become good at getting direction and following it. The results were Maury's.

This culture developed my managerial skills, but it didn't help my leadership skills. Leadership means having an idea, developing it, overseeing it, and taking responsibility for its outcome. When you see people get severely disciplined—including publicly—for having and trying a new idea, it completely squashes all creative thinking and the willingness to take risks. It's easy to see the impact this would have on a fast-growing organization.

In Maury's case, he held his people to his standard, even if they didn't think or manage like he did. In my case, instead of allowing those under me to have ideas, develop them, implement them, and measure them, I was held responsible for not identifying and stopping any problem before it actually happened. This made my environment stressful. For instance, rather than give a department leader a budget and hold him accountable if he exceeded it, I would be held responsible for not predicting and stopping the department leader *before* he actually exceeded it. Again, in a small organization, this may be possible, but in a larger organization, it's impossible. Unless you strangle people with limitless questions and are involved in every detail of everything they're doing, you can't possibly predict their behavior ahead of time.

Not only is it nearly impossible to devote this much time and financial oversight to every department and employee, but if you actually do it, you undermine their creativity by smothering them. My philosophy was, "You know your budget. If you go over, we'll discuss the ramifications." However, Maury viewed my philosophy as "not caring" or "not working hard enough" to identify every problem ahead of time.

In a micromanagement environment, most decisions are made by one individual, so the mood of that individual dictates how people respond to particular situations. Stress, anxiety, and fatigue all play a role in how the leader responds. This was particularly true in Maury's case. Like any good leader, he took things personally. He got upset over little things, which made the rest of us feel like we were walking on eggshells ... or worse, land mines. Because of my relationship with Maury, people often came by my office, cracked the door open, stuck their head in, and asked, "Is the temperature good today for me to present my idea?"

I was Maury's thermometer!

After being at the church for only a week, I discovered how important timing was, so over the next 14 years, I adapted my management style. As the CFO, it was my job to approve all purchases before they were made. In my second week, Maury flew to New Mexico to spend some time away. His instructions to me were to call him daily and run the purchasing requests by him one by one. He would make the decisions while giving me reasons for each one. On day two of his trip, I had approximately 15 requests from various departments. A major problem had just arisen with a member of our church, and Maury was quite upset about it. The first three requisitions I presented him over the phone were shot down ... and shot down hard. The requests seemed perfectly logical to me, but I quickly realized Maury's decisions were a reflection of his mood.

After the third request, he said, "Next." I responded, "That's all the requests today, sir." The following day, when Maury called, I told him that the situation with the member of the church had died down somewhat. I decided to try something: I presented the same three purchasing requests as the day before. Maury's response to all three was a resounding "yes." As you can guess, so were the additional 12 requests that I presented that day. There were many times I held things—sometimes far too long—to try and catch him in a "reasonable" mood. I knew that, when he was in a "reasonable" mood, he would make "reasonable" decisions. I never used this in a manipulative fashion; I simply wanted to give each decision its fair chance to be considered by Maury.

An additional characteristic of micromanagers is that they seldom give praise or appreciation to those on their teams. In one way, this makes perfect sense: A micromanager thinks that success or failure literally rides on his or her every decision. Staff members are making sacrifices and trying to please the leader by demonstrating their own competence and dedication, but it's never enough. While some people don't need the praise of the leader, I've found that appreciation is one of the most powerful tools a leader has in their arsenal—for good when it's used and for bad when it's withheld. Without a measure of appreciation, staff members conclude that the leader only cares about the organization, not them as individuals.

I fully believe Maury's management style was what he believed was in the best interest of the church. Don't we all? We rarely make decisions we know will hurt our organizations. Therefore, we can assume the leader has the best intentions in mind. Maury worked harder than anyone I've ever known. I don't think he had much patience, and I suspect he felt like he wasn't a good developer of leaders—therefore, he tried to do it all himself. He often said, "I might not be smarter than you, but I can outwork you all day long!"

While good-intentioned, a micromanager ultimately becomes the organization's biggest and tightest lid, because it can only grow to the size that one individual can carry. Over time, this burden wears the leader down and counteracts the very things they're trying to accomplish.

—Dana Lawson, Nonprofit Executive

MY ADVICE

Let me offer a few suggestions from someone who was slow to learn the causes and effects of smothering the people I led.

1) Take time for transparent introspection.

Ask yourself the hard questions about motives. I'm talking about hidden motives and shadow purposes, not just preacher-speak about always honoring God. All of us have mixed motives. If we're not honest about them, they'll eat us alive and prevent us from being the leaders God wants us to be.

2) **Have a mentor, coach, pastor, or consultant who will ask penetrating questions and who has the guts to say things you don't want to hear.**

    Meet regularly enough to maintain continuity in the relationship and in the input. And *listen*. Gifted, wise, experienced people see things we don't. Invite this person into your life early to maximize your potential and minimize the damage you cause.

3) **Force yourself to listen.**

    Micromanagers only listen to themselves because they only trust their own judgment. In your planning, write out questions to ask individuals on your team that will draw them out. Don't jump in to correct them or even comment. Instead, say, "Tell me more about that." If they don't want to say much or they speak with an edge of anger, it may be because you haven't created a safe environment. You can start to create one by continuing to listen. Speak last, not first. If you always have to have the first word and the last word, you'll always micromanage.

4) **Apologize.**

    If you recognize a pattern of not trusting people, of being too involved in their lives and ministries, and of robbing them of the joy of taking risks and seeing success, swallow hard and apologize. It's not enough to say, "I'm sorry," and then go back to the same oppressive routine. Combine contrition with a commitment to trust them more fully and an invitation for them to tell you when you're overstepping.

5) **Change your metrics of success.**

Instead of everything revolving around your identity as a successful pastor, push the evaluation down and broaden it: A new definition of success is your staff members' creativity, their willingness to take risks, the growth of their ministries, and the leaders they raise up and believe in. It's perfectly fine to give someone a goal, but then let him or her come up with a plan and run it by you. If you see holes in the plan, don't fill them with your directives. Point out the need and ask the person to think, pray, and complete the plan. In this way, you stay involved, but you communicate trust in the staff member's creativity and competence ... and that goes a long way to create a healthy culture. This style of leadership is coaching instead of smothering. Be a coach, not a tiger mom.

Micromanaging gifted people had multiplied negative effects. To change, I had to do a deep dive into my motives. I wish I'd done it years ago. I would have saved a lot of people a lot of heartache. But, better late than never.

CHAPTER 2

I STOPPED PURSUING FORMAL EDUCATION

*"The capacity to learn is a gift; the ability to learn is
a skill; the willingness to learn is a choice."*
—Brian Herbert

I have an associates' degree. I studied at the Berean School of the
Bible, and I participated in the Sunset School of Preaching. When
I got out, I immediately joined Pastor George at Calvary. In the years
since, I've gone to countless conferences, seminars, and workshops,
but I didn't pursue any advanced learning opportunities. Please don't
misunderstand: I didn't stop learning. I'm an avid reader—it's just
that I've invested my time reading books that interest me. In graduate
programs, students are forced to study topics outside their comfort

zones, stretching them to think more broadly and deeply and helping them to acquire insights they wouldn't have gained any other way. I missed that opportunity—or, to be more accurate, I didn't pursue it.

NARROW OR BROAD

From the time I entered ministry, my self-directed study was prompted primarily by sermon preparation. I read all kinds of books on theology, spiritual formation, and leadership. More recently, my involvement with Dream Releaser Coaching has forced me to wade into new topics. For instance, one of the required readings is an extensive book on Christian counseling. It was a grind for me. I wondered why it was so hard to get through, and realized that I hadn't read anything outside my comfort zone for decades. However, the book was terrifically helpful in opening my eyes to insights about myself and others.

Formal education gives people a more finely-tuned reasoning process. Research forces them to consider various sides of an issue in such a way that they sift through competing narratives and synthesize the best of what they find. This process protects their destiny. As I know very well, it doesn't take many dumb mistakes in judgment to run a life offtrack. A formal education gives people the tools to think more clearly, analyze more specifically, and make better decisions. I'm intuitive, so as a pastor, I instinctively made a lot of good decisions. However, I would have been more consistent, and I would have understood the reasons behind my decisions more fully, if I'd had a stronger academic foundation.

Leaders make the best decisions when there's a blend of intuition, information about risks and rewards, advice from gifted people, and intentionality to deliver the desired outcomes. For decades, I made almost all of my decisions based on intuition alone. I seldom stopped long enough to bring experts to the table to analyze processes and predict results. I just relied on my "sense of things." I got away with a lot because my intuition let me see when I needed to turn on a dime to fix a problem that was about to surface. Other people may not have seen it, but I did. On the other hand, a person who'd done research and was better informed may not have started on the initial path, so he would have avoided the problem from the outset.

Another problem for intuitive leaders is that they're hard to follow. They can go from one place to another by an internal sense of dead reckoning; most people need a map. Quite often, the rest of the team had no idea how I came up with a decision, and I wasn't good at explaining how I'd arrived at it, either. My sense of what we ought to do was clear to me, but not at all to them.

A friend of mine once asked me, "Isn't intuition the exact opposite of micromanaging? How can you do both at the same time?"

I replied, "It's a gift, brother!"

Seriously, the two traits act independently. My sense of intuition gives me an understanding of what needs to happen and the ability to anticipate outcomes. With that insight, I can either communicate my observations, delegate, and trust people, or I can micromanage every detail to make sure I get exactly what I want.

That doesn't mean a leader shouldn't be involved in things that will ultimately produce division. For instance, a man in our church started a country-boy Bible study. He was a popular person, and dozens of men were soon attending. I had a sense that the people going felt they were becoming a church unto themselves. A large percentage of Bible studies that start with the right heart end up becoming an isolated part of the church, believing they're more spiritual than other people. I talked to the men about it. Our conversation wasn't tense, but they disagreed with my assessment. At that point, my intuition was finished, and I kicked my penchant for micromanaging into overdrive.

I contacted key influencers attending the Bible study to encourage them to stop going. As you might imagine, this approach caused far more division than it solved. Instead, I could have gone to the Bible study, expressed my desire for it to be a vital part of the church, and it would have been a huge win for everybody. If I'd collaborated more with the leaders, I believe we could have worked things out so everyone was satisfied and happy with the results. But again, I was too overbearing. My intuition about the Bible study and the division it would cause between members in the church was correct, but my method could have been different.

> *"Educating the mind without educating*
> *the heart is no education at all."*
> —Aristotle

In a graduate course on leadership, I would have learned the art and science of exercising authority without becoming authoritarian. It's too bad I didn't get that … too bad for everybody.

I'm not suggesting that a specific degree is the solution to the problem I'm identifying in this chapter. Titles aren't extremely important. I know plenty of people with letters after their names who aren't exceptionally successful. There's something much more important than letters. Continuing my formal education would have changed my thought patterns, which would have given me a greater understanding of how to lead people and would have reduced my number of misguided decisions. All of us make mistakes, but I believe a richer, deeper, longer period of study would have significantly reduced the number I made. Also, this kind of academic exercise would have given me a broader range of connections with smart people who would have sharpened me and my skills. Rigorous study would have forced me to reconsider my long-held assumptions. That's an uncomfortable but necessary process. It would have made me a better leader.

Of course, I compounded this mistake because I didn't point my people toward higher learning. In my leadership style, I probably told some of them, "You don't need to go to school to get an advanced education. I'll tell you everything you need to know!" I'm not sure if I said that to anyone, but I wouldn't be surprised if I did.

WHAT COULD HAVE BEEN

I believe more rigorous academic training would have dramatically and positively impacted the development of our church. We grew until my ability to control everything found its limits. If I'd had more education, and a better grasp of leadership dynamics, I think I would have moved from micromanagement to empowerment.

Years ago, U-Haul trucks had a governor on the engines so no one could take them above, say, 60 miles an hour. No matter how far you depressed the gas pedal, the truck would only go so quickly. I was the governor on the speed of our church's growth—and by the time I realized it, we were almost out of gas.

A few years ago, I read *The Seven Pillars of Health* by Dr. Don Colbert, and I required our entire staff team to go through the exercise, sleep, and nutrition regimen in the book. We purged our offices of all the candy we enjoyed, and we had the vending companies remove the soft drink machines. I hired a trainer and required our team to meet at the gym at 6:00 AM every morning. I only half-jokingly told them, "If at least one of you doesn't throw up every day, you aren't trying hard enough." We kept track of each person's muscle mass, body weight, heart rate, and blood pressure. We made a commitment (Well, I made their commitment for them.) to be disciplined in all of Dr. Colbert's advice for six weeks. At the end, several people told me, "Pastor, this has changed my life!" It changed the culture of our team. We had more energy, we knew each other outside the office, and we saw genuine tenacity in every person on the team. We respected one another more than ever.

You might ask what this experience in physical health has to do with formal education. Here's the point: How would it have affected our team if I'd been as passionate about their brains as I was about their bodies? What if our team had studied a book like *The Speed of Trust* by Stephen Covey? I think it's pretty safe to assume that the people on my team would have expected me to trust them to make more of their own decisions—and maybe even to give input without demanding ritualistic compliance.

I had always mistakenly believed that people have rigid limits on their talents, so I didn't give them room to grow. I didn't provide an environment that stimulated personal growth and skill development. What was I thinking? Didn't I have any grasp that God could empower someone to be and do far more than anyone—specifically I—had ever dreamed possible? Why wasn't my hope in the exponential power of God instead of in my petty ability to control? I believe I would've been a far better leader if I'd pursued more academic training … not to brag about a title, but to stretch my thinking and expand my horizons. I would have thought more deeply, seen more clearly, and led with more wisdom.

In some church circles, I've seen an anti-academic bent. In one way, I understand this resistance because some arenas of academia are bastions of liberal theology, and this is also true in many seminaries. But many fine, godly schools are equipping people to serve God with a powerful grasp of His truth. Education doesn't come just in the form of college. Plenty of CEOs never went to university, but they all share an absolute passion for learning. Warren Buffet reads 500 pages a day. Mark Cuban reads for three hours a day. Bill Gates reads a book a week. Elon Musk taught himself to build rockets from books. The most successful people in the world are filling their minds with the ideas and theories of experts in the field without ever leaving a room. The endgame isn't a degree—the goal is to become a life-long learner.

As I look at successful churches and get to know their staff teams, I've noticed that professionally-trained men and women (especially in technology, creative fields such as music, and administration) operate at a higher level than those who don't have this kind of input. That's not universally true, but it usually is. I know some terrific pastors who don't have advanced degrees, but the smart ones *hire* people who do. In this new age of digital communication, pastors can make awful decisions because they simply aren't trained. I know a young pastor who determined that wearing black would be his dress code. He dressed in black, and he created a black background for his stage. In videos, he looked like a face with disembodied hands moving around. He hired a professional media company to help him, and they immediately gave him the knowledge he needed. I had my own ideas too; but at some point I realized that, if I had brought professionals into our church to offer me their expertise, I'd have been a better leader. I would have used their brains, and I would have looked a lot smarter myself.

Here's another problem: Far too often, pastors are too busy, distracted, or, in some cases, too lazy to dig deeply into intellectual pursuits. God spoke through the prophet Hosea to warn the Israelite people in this regard:

> My people are destroyed for lack of knowledge. Because you have rejected knowledge, I also will reject you from being My priest. Since you have forgotten the law of your God, I also will forget your children. (Hosea 4:6)

We won't be destroyed by a lack of grace, but we can be destroyed by a lack of knowledge. When we're too sloppy or too arrogant to learn something new, we may be disqualified from our position as shepherds of God's flock. Our lack of knowledge will leave us building sandcastles instead of churches devoted to God that will last. Our family goes to the beach for a week every summer, and another family—a large family—always comes at the same time and stays near us. The parents, grandparents, and 15 to 20 kids of all ages play in the water and build sandcastles every day. And every morning, what they spent so much time building has vanished with the night's tide. I want to go over and ask, "Don't you have knowledge that your sandcastles don't last?" But I don't. Gail won't let me.

> *"Education is not learning of facts, but the*
> *training of the mind to think."*
> —Albert Einstein

Jim Kubic realized the value of pursuing more knowledge. He was a career law enforcement officer who gave his life to Christ at Cornerstone Church. Through the process of discipleship, he felt called to ministry and eventually landed on our pastoral team. We helped him launch a church plant, and his ministry has borne great fruit.

I WAS 41 YEARS OLD when I started my Master of Divinity program at Liberty University, where I felt compelled to acquire my degree in

Pastoral Ministry. I was working a full-time ministry position at my home church, Cornerstone in Nashville, pastored by Maury Davis. He self-identified as a "buffalo leader," meaning that he led with authority, intentionality, from the front, and—when necessary—aggressively. Working for Pastor Davis was a challenge in and of itself, with a schedule that often required more than 50 hours a week.

Not only was he a pastor who led with authority and high expectations—he was also regularly vocal about the fact that a formal education wasn't really important. I can remember him saying something like, "Look at what I've been able to accomplish, and I haven't gone to college." Due to this statement, his work expectations, and his leadership style, I kept the fact that I was going through seminary a secret—at least, I thought it was a secret.

In late 2014, I began feeling a call to plant a church. In early 2015, after much prayer, I went to Pastor Maury and asked for his counsel, prayers, and, if possible, his blessing. After listening to my dream, one of the things he said to me was that he would support me and give me his blessing "provided you finish your education first." I was taken aback. I hadn't realized he knew (or if he did know, I didn't realize he cared) about me going to school. However, what I hadn't realized is that, at some point between the time I started working for him and this mandate, due to circumstances that aren't my business to share, he came to a place in his own life where an education became important. Little did I know that he, too, had begun to self-evaluate and apply himself to an education at a level higher than he'd ever previously attempted.

At the time, Pastor Davis wasn't aware that I was within a couple days of discontinuing the pursuit of my degree. I wasn't scheduled to finish my degree until mid-2016, and I wanted to plant the church in January of 2016. I had to make a choice about where I would focus my energies, and I was choosing planting over learning—not because I didn't think a higher education was important, but because I didn't think I would have time to study and plant a church. However, his mandate made me rethink my decision.

I accepted Pastor Maury's challenge, and I was forced to double up on classes for the last two semesters. It was the only way I could finish under his deadline. I look back now and, admittedly, it irritated me a little bit that he would require such a thing of me. But now I'm grateful. If he hadn't pushed me to complete my degree first, I probably never would have finished. I'm grateful for a pastor who, because of his own willingness to self-evaluate, pushed me to finish my education.

My congregation and I are better off for it. Because of his mandate, I'm a better leader, I have a greater ability to articulate complex truths, and I'm able to meet resistance from others with a sense of humility and confidence instead of defensiveness.

Thank you, Pastor Maury, for seeing what I was unable to see at the time: An education is important.

—*Jim Kubic, Senior Pastor, Launchpoint*
Church, Lebanon, Tennessee

MY ADVICE

I'm not suggesting all pastors quit their jobs and enroll in masters- or doctoral-level academic pursuits, but we can integrate classes and courses into our regular schedules to sharpen us. Here are some suggestions:

1) **At least once a year—and preferably twice a year—invest in a curriculum that promises to push you to think more deeply.**
   When I became acquainted with Dream Releaser Coaching, I was hooked in the first track. It was an easy choice to enroll in the rest of the tracks, and the teaching has greatly enriched my life. Of course, there are some seasons in a church's life when pastors don't have the bandwidth to add coursework, but it's an easy out to claim that this is true all the time.

2) **Choose wisely.**
   Many Christian colleges and seminaries have courses you can take on-site if you're nearby or online if you're not. Organizations like Dream Releaser Coaching make it easy to tap into their resources. Find courses that overlap with your interests in Christian leadership and the areas in which you need to broaden your knowledge. Christian psychology is an area that has pushed me a lot, but it's been well worth it. In other words, find courses that stimulate you but that aren't necessarily your frontline resources for sermon prep. (I highly recommend

Dream Releaser Coaching. Their training equips people with insights and relational skills.)

3) Become a student of history.

The first history professor I had in prison was a classic. He looked the part, sounded the part, and acted the part. He began by explaining that he wasn't a Christian, but we couldn't understand American history unless we looked through the lens of the Christian influence of our founders. He explained how the Reformation swept through northern Europe and changed the culture—how the first settlers in the New World came to establish God's kingdom on earth, and how the Bible became the foundation of our legal system. I was riveted on every word. My second history professor had a very different perspective. He taught us how Christians had supported slavery, how they had been hypocrites in the treatment of American Indians, and how they'd oppressed the poor in the cities. I enjoyed one and cringed at the other, but I realized they were both right. There are, in fact, two sides of the story.

4) Develop a filter.

When people study a subject and hear different sides, those without strong convictions are often bewildered and shaken. We need a strong grid so we can sift the good from the bad—or, as I often put it, "eat the hay and leave the sticks." Horses don't refuse to eat when they find sticks in their feed. They simply move them aside and keep eating the hay. Some fields, such as psychology and sociology, can teach us a lot about human thought and behavior, even if they're taught by unbelievers. However, we need to spit out the concepts that are blatantly anti-God when we run across them. If we look, we'll find brilliant Christians who teach virtually any subject. I'm not suggesting that we only listen to believers—we also need to understand what people outside the church are thinking—but it's good to have a bedrock of godly men and women as resources for our intellectual growth.

The ultimate authority, the ultimate truth, is God's Word. As we broaden our mental capacities and expose our minds to teachers, we need to remember that, if there's conflict between what we're hearing and the truth of the Scriptures, we stick with the Scriptures.

CHAPTER 3

I WAS INSENSITIVE TO PEOPLE'S FEELINGS

"It takes something more than intelligence to act intelligently."
—Fyodor Dostoyevsky

When something around the house breaks, I fix it. But people aren't appliances.

Everything is created to accomplish something. Unfortunately, I'm afraid that's how I saw people who reported to me: They were tools to achieve the purposes God had put on my heart. It wasn't just that I assigned them lanes to run in; I put them into pigeonholes and insisted they stay there. This is a painful chapter in this book … for me to write and, I would imagine, for you to read.

I trained people to stop thinking. Though I was committed to excellence, I trained my team to believe they were incapable of excellence without me hovering over them and telling them how to do everything.

In recent years, I've been able to reflect on all of this. I was raised by a harsh stepfather, I attended military academy, and I was in prison for over eight years, living in an extremely strict structure. In all of those experiences, no one in authority hesitated to correct me because they were worried about hurting my feelings. At the academy, every detail of every day was regimented. In the first year, we had to sit at attention from 7:00 to 9:00 PM every night to study. They gave us a 10-minute break at 8:00, but the rest of the time, I sat with my back ramrod straight, not touching the back of the chair. When we ate, we had to bring the fork up at a right angle to our mouths. No officer ever asked, "Maury, does this make you feel uncomfortable?" They didn't care. Well ... that's not exactly true. They cared about breaking us down and molding us into the image of a completely compliant cadet. If we put a bite in our mouths that required chewing, they called us out and gave us something to *really* chew on and swallow—like a huge dollop of peanut butter coated with mustard. The upperclassmen ordered us to do push-ups for even the most minor infraction ... and sometimes, when there was no infraction. We internalized all of this and learned that being motivated by fear was entirely normal.

Then, I went to prison. It made my time at the military academy feel like a day at the beach. Guards and other inmates weren't the least bit sympathetic, and we learned quickly (like, immediately) to avoid showing any emotion except anger. Anything that made us appear vulnerable, such as hurt, fear, guilt, or grief, put a target on our backs. It became a matter of survival: Real men never break, and they never even show a crack.

For my entire life, up to the time I became a pastor, I lived in a man's world where we regularly called each other names. It was a sign of acceptance. If no one called you fat or dumb or ugly, you weren't part of the group. This brand of "acceptance" is based only on sarcasm and put-downs. When I became a pastor, I was still more institutional than pastoral, but I had a good and noble goal: the Great Commission. I didn't know how to communicate tenderness and support. I only understood the law of the jungle and pressured people to do God's will. I instilled and inflamed their fear to coerce them to perform. My words and my tone were clear: I cared about performance, not feelings. I really did care about them and their families, but my training had created a bully—not a friend.

For the people on our team, the consequences of delay or failure were crystal clear. They'd seen me yell at people, and they'd seen me belittle people in front of everyone. That was my experience in military school, and it was how things were done in prison. I hadn't yet made the switch to a church culture.

HUMILIATION AS MOTIVATION

Mark Lunsford joined us as our Music Pastor. That was his slot: music. I didn't see (and I didn't look for) the range of talents and gifts he possessed. He wanted to come to Nashville because the pool of talent is incredibly deep in Music City, USA. Many churches have professional performers on the stage every Sunday. Mark has a real talent to organize musicians and singers, but singing isn't one of his strengths. One week, at a staff meeting, I asked him, "Why did you sing that part in the song Sunday night?" I'd gone to the trouble to single out his part in the recording, and I played it in front of everybody. I told him, "I'm sure you put yourself in there because someone didn't show up. You were horrible. You embarrassed me."

He was completely humiliated, but I kept pressing my point: "I don't want you singing into a microphone again unless you're in your vocal range. You may be the Minister of Music, but you're not the main worship leader." I felt completely justified in treating Mark this way, and I believed I'd been doubly effective because everyone saw the consequences of failing to live up to my expectations.

For my entire life, I'd learned to get over things quickly. A stern correction may hurt me for a minute or two, but no longer than that. I assumed other people were like me. They weren't, and they aren't. I thought I was training Mark and helping him, but I hurt him deeply. Mark is a gifted leader, but I didn't see it.

I remember walking by his office one day and noticing that he was just sitting there. I stopped at his door and asked, "What are you doing?"

He said, "Just thinking."

My blood boiled. I snarled, "I don't pay you to think. I pay you to work!"

It was a really dumb thing to say, but it's even worse that I believed it. People who micromanage have two related, devastating effects: They communicate to people that they're incompetent, and they create an environment of fear so people always wait on them, the leader, to make every decision. They haven't felt valued or free to speak up, so they wither away in a drought of affirmation.

After that tense moment in his office, I made sure Mark had plenty of things on his list every day. However, after a week or so, when I passed by his office, I saw that he was just sitting there again. When I stopped at his door, I'm sure the expression on my face wasn't exactly full of kindness. I sneered, "Mark, what are you doing?"

"Thinking."

Man, I was really upset. I barked, "I told you that I want you to work, not think!"

Without missing a beat, he informed me, "Pastor, I had a number of things on my list, and right now, four people are accomplishing them. Tomorrow, they're turning in a report on their progress. Don't worry. I'll be sure they do it like we want it done."

That wasn't good enough for me. I told him, "I'm sick of you just sitting around. I want you to work."

He explained, politely, "Pastor, the goal is to get all this done. I'm doing everything that's on my list, but I'm doing it through these people."

I had the bone in my teeth, and I wasn't going to let it get away. "But you're not working!"

Mark has the gift of administration. He can think through things and find ways to involve gifted people to accomplish far more than they would have on their own. He created the first small groups at our church in the choir so that he could be sure their spiritual and emotional needs were met as they served the church each week. However, after the way I'd treated him, I'm afraid Mark drew the only logical conclusion: It wasn't safe to be around me. He withdrew and took fewer risks so he could avoid public humiliation. His creativity wilted, and he was afraid to even give input because he didn't want to be blasted again. He noticed the songs I liked, and he used them more often than he would have if he'd felt free to pick from a wider range. I'm pretty sure his primary goal was getting through each day without getting in trouble with me. Instead of being a difference-maker, he became a defensive player.

Mark was with us for more than six years, but I never gave him room to use his remarkable talents. When he left Cornerstone, he became the executive pastor at Hope Fellowship in Frisco, Texas, and now at Orchard Hill Church in Pittsburgh Pennsylvania—he has been the secret sauce to build great churches in those locations. My micromanaging severely limited what Mark did at Cornerstone, and my lack of sensitivity drove him away. My leadership flaw was detrimental to him, to his ministry, and to the church. If I'd seen his extraordinary talents and encouraged him to spread his wings and fly, there's no telling how God might have used him in our church. Thankfully, God put him in a place where he was free to be creative, free to take risks, free to fail, and free to see incredible success. I'm just sorry he had to leave me for that to happen.

I'll let him tell his side of the story.

❦ • • • ❦

I CAME TO CORNERSTONE WHEN I was 24 from a pretty secure family and a good church background. My family experiences and my first job in ministry were empowering and encouraging. I wanted to please the people over me, but not because I was needy. I wanted to honor them.

Maury was skeptical of people who reported to him. It seemed that his primary question, if he'd voiced it, would have been, "What are you trying to get away with?" That's the opposite of my motivation. Actually, I'm not good at playing mind games and manipulating people, but Maury is an expert. When I failed at something, he assumed I'd done it to spite him. In almost every case, it was my ignorance, not rebellion, that caused the problem. I wanted to please and support him, but nothing I did was ever good enough.

On a Sunday night about two years into my time at the church, I had someone sing "A Place Called Hope" in our service. At the time, Bill Clinton was the president, and Maury thought the song was too supportive of Clinton. (Clinton is from Hope, Arkansas.) Immediately after the service, I was with about a hundred choir members. Maury stormed up to me. He was steaming mad. He seethed, "I don't ever want to hear that song again! If I do, I'll fire you on the spot!"

I don't think anyone in the choir had ever seen this side of him. The people in our choir loved me and respected me. They couldn't believe Maury would treat me that way, especially in front of them. I was stunned. We never sang that song again, but the experience put me over the edge. That night when I got home, I told my wife, Ann, "I don't think we're supposed to be here. There's something really wrong about all of this. How could this be the place where God wants me when I try so hard to please Maury but nothing works? I'm banging my head against his wall. After tonight, I have nowhere to go. I'm going to resign."

The next morning, I went to his office and told him, "I apologize. I never would have scheduled that song if I'd known you felt so strongly about it. I'm not giving you what you need, so I need to give you my resignation."

Maury told me, "I don't think you should resign. There's a lot left for you to do here at Cornerstone, and I think we can work together. We'll both learn to communicate better. I'm not going to accept your resignation. Go home and tell Ann you're going to stay. We'll work this out." It wasn't exactly an apology, but that's how I took it. So I stayed.

Actually, this was a turning point in my relationship with Maury. I think he was impressed that I'd stood up to him and that I was willing to leave. My integrity and sense of honor were more important than my job, and he respected me for that. Our relationship was different from that day on—it wasn't great, but it was better.

Part of what made it crazy to be around Maury was that those of us on the staff team never knew which Maury was going to show up that day. If it were "Happy Maury," it was the greatest day we could imagine. But if it were "Angry Maury," we had to steer clear.

I had to learn to communicate better with Maury. At any time of any day, he would walk into my office and ask, "What are you doing?" I knew this wasn't a casual question. He was checking up on me. I think his "leadership love language" is accomplishment, but I didn't learn to speak it until after I left. I was leading a creative ministry, so my "what's next" often involved collaborating with people—building leaders. Those goals and processes didn't always translate into bullet points on a to-do list, so when Maury asked the question, he assumed I wasn't working hard enough.

After several years, it became apparent that Maury and I weren't on the same page with the music at Cornerstone. It was time for me to go—and thankfully, it was an amicable parting. Long after I'd left the church, Maury told me that the systems and processes I'd implemented were still helping the church grow. That was good to hear, but I wish he'd realized that while I was there.

—*Mark Lunsford, Executive Director, Orchard*
Hill Church, Pittsburgh Pennsylvania

❧ • • • ❧

"Anybody can become angry; that is easy. But to become
angry with the right person and to the right degree and at
the right time and for the right purpose and in the right way,
that is not within everybody's power and is not easy."
—Aristotle

OTHER PEOPLE WHO JOINED OUR team quickly experienced the damage they'd endure if they didn't please me, so they made sure to never step out of line. Still, I wasn't cruel all the time. I was Dr. Jekyll and Mr. Hyde. When team members came over to our house or we did something else together, I was the life of the party. After I went through DRC training, I talked to some of them. One person told me, "When I walked into the office in the morning and looked at the expression on your face, I knew if it was safe to be me or if I needed to hide." He paused and asked, "Why do you think we closed our doors?"

I replied, "I have no idea."

He explained, "If you were mad about anything and we were in your line of sight, we were in trouble."

On my best days, I was determined and driven, but I was encouraging to people around me. I could go into someone's office and chat for an hour. Now, I wonder what they were thinking. Probably, *Is this the calm before the storm?*

Then, I had a lot of bad days. I didn't trust many people. Only those who were exemplary performers earned my approval. One day, I told our team to line up against the wall in the back of the room. They may have thought I was a one-man firing squad. Honestly, they weren't far off. I gave them orders: "Phil, Joe, and Alice, stand over here." They moved to the spots where I pointed. "Janice, James, Rachel, and Rita, stand there." They moved to the place where I directed them. "The rest of you, stay where you are." I turned to the first group and asked, "What's the most common question I ask you?"

One of them responded, "You ask, 'How are you doing?' and 'What can I do to help you?'"

I turned to the second group and asked, "What is the question I ask you most often?"

In a few seconds, one of them said, "You always ask, 'When are you going to get that assignment finished?' and 'Is there anything you need from me to get it done?'"

I asked the third group, "And what do I often ask you?"

They looked at each other, and finally, one of them said, "Well, you always ask, 'What did you accomplish today?' 'What's on your calendar?' and 'What's taking you so long?'"

I had more trust for the first group than the second, and more for the second than the third. In this exercise—and, I'm sure, in every other staff meeting—I communicated that the third group was "less than," "not as sharp as," and "can't do anything without my attention and prodding." I had a lot of confidence in a few, some confidence in many, and very little in the rest.

To drive the point home, I told the first group, "I never get complaints from people in the church about you. You always do what you say you'll do, and you do it well. You are high performers who have gotten the job done over a long period of time." I turned to the other two groups and said only, "But I get calls about you …" I didn't need to say another word. Parents had come to me voicing concerns about the youth group or children's ministry, and other people in the church had called or sent emails complaining that a staff member had dropped the ball. I didn't trust this group because they had failed, and in my perfectionism, failure—for them and for me, because their performance was a reflection of me—was totally unacceptable. My reaction was bad if staff members came to me before I got the call or the email, but it was exponentially worse if the church member's call or email came first. I lived with a daunting sense of skepticism. I was sure the other shoe would drop any day: The second group *might* mess up, and the third group *would* mess up. This level of suspicion is an inmate's perspective of people, and it was still mine.

I realized the questions I asked each group showed my level of trust in them and how little I'd moved them from merely being employed by the church to becoming people responsible for exercising spiritual authority. Sadly, I didn't come to this realization until very late in my career as a pastor; even more sadly, I used this shaming exercise to show them what I'd discovered.

Our culture has shifted from relying on IQ to EQ and now to EI: Emotional Intelligence, which is the ability to perceive, control, and evaluate emotions. In 1995, Dr. Daniel Goleman proposed that there are four domains of emotional intelligence: self-awareness, self-management, social awareness (empathy), and relationship management (social skills).[2]

SELF-AWARENESS	SELF-MANAGEMENT	SOCIAL AWARENESS	RELATIONSHIP MANAGEMENT
Know your story and how it affects you.	Develop skills for breathing and relaxation.	Understand nonverbal communication.	Develop skills for reflective listening and empathy.
Make peace with your past.	Learn positive, self-affirming beliefs.	Develop a positive view of others.	Develop skills for assertive communication.
Know your beliefs, emotions, and behavior patterns.	Develop self-soothing and self-motivation skills.	Understand the basic emotional needs.	Learn conflict resolution skills.
Know your relationship patterns.	Maintain good physical health.	Understand "games" and personal integrity.	Learn skills for support and affirmation of others.

I had an EQ, but I didn't have emotional intelligence. As I went through the consulting process with Dr. Chand, I began to develop self-awareness. I dove deeply into my past to understand why I was the way I was. Now, I've learned to manage myself: to anticipate and prepare my reactions in order to deal with people more effectively and more lovingly. This allows me to be aware of and show grace to

2 Daniel Goleman, "Emotional Intelligence," April 21, 2015, http://www.danielgoleman.info/daniel-goleman-how-emotionally-intelligent-are-you/.

those around me, which will strengthen my management of relationships in the future.

We don't really need to turn to the Scriptures to see that abusive behavior is totally wrong. We know it when we see it, and we *really* know it when we're the victims of it. I believe God has put a sense of justice in the heart of every person—believers and unbelievers—but we can become so twisted that we care more about a person's achievements than the person.

People aren't dishwashers to be fixed or thrown away. In one of King David's most beautiful psalms, he marvels that the God of creation formed him:

> I will give thanks to You, for I am fearfully and wonderfully made; Wonderful are Your works, And my soul knows it very well. (Psalm 139:14)

Every person has been created in the image of God and is a treasure. His handiwork shaped us inside and out, and He has given us dignity and honor. I'm afraid this truth hadn't penetrated my soul well enough. Jesus told us, "In everything, therefore, treat people the same way you want them to treat you, for this is the Law and the Prophets" (Matthew 7:12). Did I want people to treat me like a tool or like a beloved person and a partner in ministry? Actually, I felt more comfortable being treated like a tool. I'd done some very bad things and, deep in my heart, I didn't think I deserved better. But I'm not the victim in all of this. I'm the victimizer.

Jesus always treated people with the utmost respect—those who ridiculed Him, those who didn't understand Him, and even those who hated Him. He didn't run over them to accomplish His mission ... they *were* His mission!

I had to learn that there's a difference between a scheme and a dream. A scheme only benefits me at the expense of others; a dream fulfilled has a positive impact on everybody.

MY ADVICE

I hope no one reading this is as harsh and demanding as I've been. If I've earned a hearing by my honesty, allow me to offer some suggestions.

1) Remember that we're in the people business.

It's too easy to believe that numbers determine our success and value as leaders. But no matter how big our churches grow, if the people closest to us don't feel loved and encouraged—especially when they fail—we've missed the mark as God's under-shepherds. The church isn't a prison, and it's not a corporation. It's Christ's body, and it can't be healthy unless its leaders build up instead of tearing down. When I read the Gospels, I see Jesus stop to care for people again and again. He had the highest goal anyone has ever embraced, but His goal wasn't numbers; it was people. It still is.

2) Have the courage to look inside.

This is a common theme in this book: When we aren't honest about the open wounds we carry with us, every goal, every motive, and every relationship is adversely affected. I'm responsible for some of the hurts I've experienced, but I'm not responsible for others. No matter what the cause, I'm completely responsible for how I deal with them. In my pain, I was convinced that expressing any tender emotions made me look vulnerable, and I wasn't willing to let that happen. I hid my compassion behind a rough exterior because I didn't want anyone to think I was weak.

3) **Ask God to make His love more real to you than the pain of your past.**

You can't will your way out of this destructive pattern of behavior. You have to be melted in the warmth of God's affection and then remolded by the power of the Spirit. I believe God delights to answer this prayer.

4) **Learn new scripts.**

We're creatures of habit. We react to similar situations in the same way, time after time. We say the same things to the same people over and over. Take a few minutes to think about the past week, and write down the situations in which you were harsh and demanding. How did you feel? What did you say? How did you affect the people you addressed? Now, write a new script for what you *wish* you'd said each time—a message that may be just as true but that is full of grace, hope, and love. Keep that piece of paper with you. Before you go home to your family or walk into your next meeting, read the script and choose those words. You can't control how you feel, but you can control how you react.

This exercise may change your life and your close relationships.

God has worked in wonderful ways through me, and I give Him all the credit. But when I look back on my relationships with people on our staff teams, I'm heartbroken that I hurt so many so deeply. God is changing me, and all God's children are glad.

CHAPTER 4

I CONFUSED "AUTHENTIC" WITH "UNFILTERED"

*"Authentic leadership is revealed in the alignment of
what you think, what you say and what you do."*
—Michael Holland

I convinced myself that saying outlandish things made me authentic, which, as we all know, is highly prized in our culture. All kinds of research says that people want their leaders to be real, to be genuine, to be authentic. That's what I was going for. I made a habit of being sarcastic and of using humor that got a lot of laughs, but I offended a significant number of people Jesus loves. I was unfiltered, not authentic.

No place was off-limits for my brand of humor. One Sunday morning in a worship service, I made a reference to midgets. I said, "It's just a small issue."

My son, Galen, was sitting in the front row. He got my attention and in a loud whisper told me, "Dad, you can't say that!"

Since about a fourth of the people in the room heard him, I smiled and said, "That's okay, Son. It's over their heads." The place was rolling with laughter ... except for a very tall lady in the third row.

After the service, she came up to talk to me. It looked like she had her little boy with her. She wasn't smiling. Through clenched teeth, she said, "I want to talk to you."

I told her, "I don't think we've met. I'm very happy to get to know you." I started to pat her son on the head, but then I noticed he had a beard! I apologized profusely, but they never came back to Cornerstone.

In 2013, I took a motorcycle trip around the country with my youngest son. When we got back and I stood up to preach, people wanted to hear a story or two about our trip. I told them, "I have to tell you, we stayed in a lot of hotels across the country while we were gone. I don't care how many times they say, 'We'll leave the light on for you'—I'm not stopping at those hotels." The regional director for Motel 6 was in the room.

I repeated a great story as if it had happened to me. I told our congregation, "I was driving on a rainy night in Florida, and I didn't see a car that had stopped in front of me. I rear-ended it. My airbag inflated and hit me like a Mike Tyson right hook. I was dazed, but in a few seconds, I heard banging on my door. I couldn't see anybody, so I rolled down the window. A dwarf started yelling at me. I stopped him and asked, 'Which one of the seven are you?'" It appears that I didn't learn anything from my earlier off-brand comment about midgets. The place was up for grabs. There was no way to bring it back and say anything meaningful in a sermon, so I just ended the service.

When our triplets were about eight years old, Gail told me she was pregnant again. Both of us were afraid she'd have another litter. We didn't tell many people until she started showing—and by then, it was time to tell the church family. During a service, I told our people, "Y'all are part of our family, and we want you to give Gail a big hand because … she's pregnant again!" They applauded, but I couldn't leave well enough alone. I continued: "I want you to pray for me, because I'm scared to death." I paused for a second, and then told them, "You need to know that it's not my fault. If she hadn't woken me up while I was sleeping, it wouldn't have happened. But you know how she is." Gail was utterly mortified. To make it worse, the only part that was true was that she was pregnant. I had made the rest up.

Not everything is meant to be funny. One day, the police called to inform me that they'd heard of a man who was threatening to hurt one of my children to get back at me for a stance I'd taken in the community. The next Sunday, I stood onstage and told our people about the threat. Then, I explained, "I'm a husband and father before I'm a pastor. If you ever think of harming my family, I'm going to pull out my inner inmate, and I'll beat you like a stepchild right out here in the parking lot!" The people gave me a standing ovation, but John

McKenzie sat there thinking, *There's something very wrong with this church when the pastor talks about beating somebody up and gets a standing ovation.*

WHY IN THE WORLD?

Authentic is predictable and positive; *unfiltered* is totally unpredictable and hurts as many as it helps. Plenty of people loved my humor, but they instinctively understood that it limited the people they wanted to invite to Cornerstone. In other words, my humor limited the people who might have come to hear God's Word.

A friend asked me what prompted me to be so unfiltered. I had to think long and hard about it. Like many of our motivations, it's complicated. I grew up listening to Don Rickles. He made a career out of sarcasm, and no ethnic group was off-limits. He wasn't subtle. His tongue was a sharp sword that sliced every intended victim: white people, black people, brown people, fat people, skinny people, pretty people, ugly people, Jewish people, Christian people, Muslim people, and on and on. He was an equal opportunity offender … and I loved it. As a pastor, this brand of humor was ingrained into my mind and heart, so it came naturally. If people were offended back then, they kept it to themselves. Another aspect of my problem is that I really don't like the limits imposed today by those who insist we should be politically correct. My unfiltered remarks have been a minor rebellion against the modern PC culture. There are two other factors that play into my motives for being unfiltered: In case you haven't noticed, I'm not the most sensitive person on God's green earth; and I find great pleasure in wit, no matter who says it—but especially when it comes from my mouth.

Terry Exley was a member of our board who then joined our pastoral staff. On a Monday morning, after I'd said something in the service the night before, I walked in while he was talking to Pastor Sandy. They were reviewing the list of unfiltered comments in just that one sermon. When he saw me, he asked, "Do you ever feel bad about anything you say?"

Instantly, I remarked, "Yes, but I get over it."

I walked on by, but I was still within earshot when I heard him say, "But other people don't."

> *"Authenticity is the daily practice of letting go of who we think we're supposed to be and embracing who we are."*
> —Brené Brown

IMPACT

To be honest, I kept saying crazy things because they drew a lot of people to our church. I'm sure those who were amused invited their friends by saying, "You've got to come. You never know what our pastor will say!" It didn't take long for me to develop a reputation as "the pastor who says whatever comes to mind." It was, I'm afraid, entirely accurate.

I didn't care that I offended the PC crowd. My appeal was to the hardworking, good-hearted men and women who have traditional values. I can relate to them. I've never had a plumber, an electrician, a carpenter, or a contractor be horrified or tell me, "Pastor, I can't believe you said that." Instead, they say, "You said exactly what I believe."

Some of our team members saw how people were hurt by my jokes and stories, and they made sure they didn't follow my example in their own communication. But a few felt free to emulate me. After one of my senior staff members gave a message on a Sunday night, a board member called me to complain about her casual use of vulgar language referring to a body part. I felt caught in the middle. It had obviously caused the board member to be concerned ... but how could I correct someone on my staff when she'd seen me do the same thing so many times before?

TURNING POINT

When our church's growth slowed to a halt in 2012, I had to face the fact that my communication was at least one of the limiting factors. I contacted Sam Chand to ask for his input. In our conversations, I realized the culture had shifted, but that I hadn't shifted with it. I had some honest talks with people I trust and love. A common theme in their feedback was that my humor was no longer a draw. In fact, it had become a barrier to growth. More than a few of them told stories of inviting people to church—their friends had been turned off by my attempts to be funny.

People who were already comfortable with my humor stayed, but few new people came. Those who had been with us for years enjoyed my unfiltered manner, but God had called us to reach far beyond our walls. I realized that you don't make fun of people you love; and if I was making fun of homosexuals or foreigners or people from different parts of our country, it was a neon flashing sign that I didn't love them. I didn't have just a mouth problem; I had a heart problem. No matter how much joy I got out of turning a witty phrase and making people laugh, love is far more important.

> *"Familiarity breeds contempt; distance brings respect."*
> —African proverb

I was treating our people like family. That doesn't sound like a bad idea, but here's what happened: It's perfectly fine for me to walk through my house wearing just my boxers if it's only Gail and me there. But, if we invite guests, it's a good idea for me to put pants on. It was time for me to put my verbal pants on.

To be honest, it's been a very hard transition for me. A couple of times a year, we have a question-and-answer time on Sunday night. I sit on a stool onstage, and a roving mic lets people ask me anything. Not long after we moved into our new building, we had one of these evenings. A lady got the mic and asked, "Pastor, can you tell us why we have these chairs instead of pews?"

I told her and everyone in the room, "Oh yeah—it's simple. If your butt hangs over onto the chair next to you, it's a signal that you need to go on a diet."

The men laughed. The women … not so much.

A few days later, a guy called to tell me that his wife had been offended by my joke. I told him I had a rule: If you laugh at my joke in the service, you can't complain about it later.

When I read the Bible, there are some passages I'd like to go over with a black highlighter. Thomas Jefferson cut out the parts of the New Testament about Jesus' miracles, and I'd like to do something like that with a few verses, too. One of them is a verse in which Jesus corrects the misconceptions of the scribes and Pharisees. He tells them,

> You brood of vipers, how can you, being evil, speak what is good? For the mouth speaks out of that which fills the heart. The good man brings out of his good treasure what is good; and the evil man brings out of his evil treasure what is evil. But I tell you that every careless word that people speak, they shall give an accounting for it in the day of judgment. For by your words you will be justified, and by your words you will be condemned. (Matthew 12:34-37)

He can't be talking about me, can He? Yes, He certainly can. Someday, I'll stand before God on the day of judgment. This isn't the "Day of the Lord," when unbelievers are cast into outer darkness. This is the judgment of believers. On that day, I'll be asked to give an account for "every careless word" I've spoken. I've said a lot of words that build people up and point them to the grace found only in Jesus; I've also said far too many careless, offensive, and hurtful words … to people Jesus loves so much that He died for them.

Another passage that sends shivers down my spine is in Paul's letter to the Ephesians:

> Let no unwholesome word proceed from your mouth, but only such a word as is good for edification according to the need of the moment, so that it will

give grace to those who hear. Do not grieve the Holy
Spirit of God, by whom you were sealed for the day of
redemption. (Ephesians 4:29-30)

He didn't say, "Cut down your hurtful words by half. That's good
enough." He said the only good and godly standard is "no unwhole-
some word"—not even *one*. But nature abhors a vacuum, so we have
to fill up that space with something. If we simply try to shut our
mouths, we'll fail. We need to speak in ways that affirm, heal, and
encourage. Paul makes the remarkable statement that our words don't
just hurt people—they hurt the Holy Spirit. The Spirit grieves in distress and sorrow when we say things that tear people down. Paul gives
us a hope and a warning: We're sealed for the day of redemption, the
day when we'll see Jesus face-to-face, welcomed into glory. At that
time, however, we'll give an account of the words we've spoken. That
may not make you think twice about unfiltered words, but it surely
does make me think twice.

The great leaders of any movement, from Gandhi to Martin Luther
King, Jr., to Hitler to Churchill, all have one thing in common: their
mastery of words. All leaders should master words—their meaning,
their intent, their reception, and their inflection. If you can control
words, you can motivate people and enact real change. There's nothing
wrong with being candid, but truth should be thoughtfully expressed
and spoken in love. Flippant speech breeds emotional reactions that
cloud productivity and distort focus and momentum.

John McKenzie was our youth pastor, worship leader, and long-
time friend, and he had a close-up view of how my communication
style caused a world of problems.

$\#$ • • • $\#$

"DAVIS, YOU CAN'T SAY THAT!"

That was my introduction to Pastor Maury Davis in a staff meeting at Calvary Temple in Irving, Texas. Little did I know how many times I'd hear that over the next ten years—first at Calvary Temple and later as Maury's youth pastor at Cornerstone Church in Madison, Tennessee. I heard it from Maury's mentor, Pastor J. Don George. I heard it from Maury's friends, co-workers, family, and church members. Maury has always been known for saying what everyone else is thinking, but what no one is willing to voice. His clear-cut, no-nonsense, take-no-prisoners, hold-on-to-your-seats style of communicating earned both rave reviews and hate mail. But love it or hate it, everyone listened.

Listening to Pastor Davis is like riding a roller coaster in a pitch-black building—you never know what twist or turn is coming next. It takes your breath away, and it might even make you scream. But when it's over, you get right back in line! There's something about the unexpected that's compelling. It's why you won't turn off a close basketball game, a WWF wrestling match, or a Maury Davis sermon. I've listened to him hundreds of times, and I still keep coming back for one more ride. Thousands agree with me. Every week, they packed the seats to hear what Pastor Davis might say next. It worked.

As exciting as listening to Pastor Davis was, there are also some challenges to that style of communication. One of the most important parts of the church is our mission—more specifically, the Great Commission. We take seriously Christ's mandate to go to all nations making disciples. Well, a huge part of our church culture in those days (and in the church I pastor today) was the importance of inviting people to come to church with you. Not everyone appreciates an unpredictable pastor. Not everyone appreciates an unfiltered communicator. Not everyone agreed with what Maury had to say, and it affected their motivation to invite people to attend a service. In other words, this style can cause someone in the church to think twice before they invite someone, because the pastor might say something that unnecessarily offends the guests.

And to be clear, I'm not talking about the fundamentals of the Christian faith or what the Word of God is very clear on; I'm talking about opinions rather than doctrine. Many times, when our opinions matter more to us than people, we lose influence. Someone with an unpredictable communication style can easily lose influence solely because of their style. Many, many times, it's not just *what* we say but *how* we say it that matters. I believe Pastor would agree with me that there were quite a few times his style got in the way of his influence.

It's my belief that, no matter your personality, leadership style, or communication style, you must intently listen to the people around you. I remember many times sitting in Pastor's office, driving in the car, or having lunch and trying desperately to give him another perspective on something we were facing—or to explain how something he'd said was offensive to people and that he should consider not saying it again. (I'm laughing while I write this because I remember so many of these conversations!) Sometimes, he listened; most of the time, he did or said whatever he wanted to do or say. If you have this kind of impulsive, unfiltered style, consider listening to the people around you. They'll help you increase your influence and further your mission—all for the glory of God.

Having said all that, the positives of Maury's unpredictable, unfiltered, blunt form of communication so often negated the challenges of that style. The first thing that comes to mind about his straightforward style was that it created a sense of clear direction and vision. People love a confident leader, and Maury was a *very* confident leader. His passion for our community and for preaching God's Word in such a candid way was unparalleled. This was attractive to the church in a pivotal season. The second thing that comes to my mind is that his style created an uncompromising culture based on God's Word. He communicated the Word of God with incredible passion, and was determined that we take God at His Word and that our desire as a church would be to live lifestyles that honor Him. This created a refreshing "no fear of what anyone might think" kind of culture, which set into motion an uncompromising vision based on God's Word.

The third thing Maury's style created was an excitement each and every weekend—you never knew what he was going to say. This might sound trivial, but it was authentic, and it created a fun atmosphere as well as a hunger for God's Word. Maury made church exciting—never boring! This again was huge in that season; there are countless messages that people will never forget because of this style!

Serving under Maury's leadership was one of the greatest seasons of growth for me as a young leader, and I will always be grateful. There were many times I had to buckle my seat belt, but he greatly influenced who I am today, how I work, and how I lead our church.

—*John McKenzie, Pastor of Hope Fellowship, Frisco, Texas*

❧ • • • ❧

MY ADVICE

It was important for me to stop making the assumption that my words didn't offend anyone, or that their entertainment benefits outweighed the hurt they caused. When I finally took time to ask, I found that my communication was far more harmful than I knew. Here are some tips from someone who has come a long way and still has a long way to go.

1) **Pay attention when people say you've hurt them.**

A few years ago, I was talking about country people, and I used the term "redneck." To me, this word referred to a Southerner who works with his hands; however, a black man told me that, in his world, the word is closely associated with white supremacists. On another occasion, I told a story about a time Gail and I went to a black-owned restaurant. I explained to our people that this was our first time there, "So I asked the black ladies what we should order." After the service, a young woman came up to me and asked, "Why did you have to say that in your story?"

I asked, "Say what?"

"Why did you have to say they were black? Why didn't you just say 'two ladies'? Are you a racist?"

I answered, "No, I'm an advocate for racial equality."

But she was incensed at what she perceived as a racist comment. She insisted, "You need to stand up next week and apologize to everybody."

I've learned two things: I need to be much more aware of how terms that were normal 20 years ago sound today, and for some people, an apology isn't good enough.

2) **Ask for feedback.**

Don't make the assumption that you aren't offending people. Have the courage to ask for honest observations, and the humility to listen without becoming defensive.

3) **Be intentional about the purpose of every message.**

I had to dig deep into my heart and ask myself, *Am I using my sermon to entertain people or to build the kingdom of God? Am I more interested in their laughter than their repentance? How will I measure success on Monday: by the number of pats on the back or the number of tears of confession and joy?* I realized that I was often getting sidetracked by my own wit. Once I started down that path, it was very hard to come back. I needed to focus on God's Word and God's heart in my preparation, prayers, and presentation, in order to avoid rabbit trails that were counterproductive to God's purposes.

4) **Value people.**

Love is more important than laughter. Our motives can get so clouded that we lose sight of what's truly important. Jesus said the world will know we're His disciples by our love for each other, and love means changing our agendas to match His—not replacing His with ours.

My brand of humor is so deeply ingrained that it has taken monumental effort and fervent prayer to change it. The people around me undoubtedly have said, "It's about time!"

CHAPTER 5

I MADE BAD STAFFING DECISIONS

"Time spent on hiring is time well spent."
—Robert Half

I'm not sure why I was so skeptical about certain aspects of the ministry but blindly optimistic about others. My assumptions about the people we hired fit in the second category. I was sure every person who joined our team would fit perfectly into our culture, display incredible skills, be amazingly humble, and "ride for the brand." What could possibly go wrong?

It's easy to make inaccurate assumptions. For instance, when we found out Gail was pregnant with triplets, I was shocked and then off-the-wall with excitement. I couldn't wait to tell my mother and father the news. My dad put a pin in my balloon when he deadpanned, "You should be glad you don't already have a child."

I asked, "Why?"

"Because you have no idea how hard this is going to be."

He was right. For months (that seemed like centuries) after the three preemie kids were born, nighttime feedings came one after the other. After I finally got a couple of hours sleep, I made 27 bottles of formula to feed them during the day. Giving them baths was an Olympian feat. At least one was crying and squirming, and sometimes all three of them acted like they were suffering torture. Our little boy seemed to wait until the exact moment I was changing their diapers to let go with assorted bodily fluids. From time to time, when Gail and I weren't completely exhausted, I thought back on those calm days before delivery and wondered, *What was I thinking?*

I've had the same thought many times when a staff hire didn't work out the way I planned. If I'd had reasonable expectations, I wouldn't have been as disappointed, but in my mind, I created a "Super Staff Person." I fully expected each one to …

- be the consummate team player
- be a high-level performer
- be amazingly teachable and humble
- match my level of passion for the church and for the cause of Christ
- have wisdom to make great decisions
- be emotionally stable, financially healthy, and relationally strong
- leave their personal problems at home each day

- anticipate the needs of people in their area of ministry
- bond with those in the church
- believe that my vision and my leadership are the best ever

Was that asking too much?

MY FIRST MISTAKE

My first hire at Cornerstone was a disaster. I'll call him Phil, and I'll call his wife Kimberly. When I interviewed him, I was so impressed that I didn't bother with a background check. Since Kimberly wasn't going to work for the church, I didn't even think of looking into her background. He was handsome, and she was beautiful. I was convinced that Phil had a heart for God, and that was good enough for me.

I offered Phil a position as our youth pastor (the only other staff position at the church). Before he accepted, he told me he needed a higher salary than I'd initially offered, in addition to living cost-free in the parsonage. The board agreed to the raise before Phil and Kimberly even walked through the door. I was convinced it was a small, additional price to pay for such a stellar couple.

In the third week of their first month, Phil and Kimberly knocked on my office door and asked to see me. He said, "Pastor, we're out of money, and we don't have anything for groceries until the first of next month."

I asked, "Did you have some moving expenses you didn't anticipate?"

"No, it's not that," he told me. "It's just not enough money for our lifestyle."

I was a bit confused. "It's the amount you asked for, isn't it? You don't have any housing expenses. What seems to be the problem?"

Kimberly jumped in. "It's just not enough money for us to live on."

I offered to help them analyze their budget, but they weren't willing for me to give them any input. Finally, I told them, "I'm going to give you $100 for groceries for the next week, but don't let this happen again."

She insisted, "That's not enough money for a week of food."

I shook my head, "Well, there are only two of you. It's more than enough for a week."

They walked out with the $100, but none of us were happy about our interaction. In the third week of their second month, Phil and Kimberly came back again. It was Groundhog Day. I knew there was no need to go through the same song and dance, so I said, "Wait right here." I went to the benevolence freezer and took out a box of 300 hot dogs, a case of buns, and bottles of ketchup and mustard. I carried them back to my office and handed it all to them. I said, "Okay, you're all set."

Kimberly was stunned and told me, "We can't eat weenies three meals a day for a week!"

I assured her, "Oh, yes, you can!"

They didn't come back for several months, but by the middle of summer, we had a different problem. One sunny day, when I got in my car to go to lunch, I noticed Kimberly sunbathing in the yard of the parsonage, which was in the middle of our church property, in full view of everyone coming and going. And she was in a bikini.

Immediately, I found Phil and told him, "Brother, this won't do. If Kimberly wants to sunbathe, she needs to go to a pool or the lake … anywhere but in front of the parsonage!"

He didn't like it, but he didn't argue. He nodded and turned to leave. About 20 minutes later, Kimberly stormed through my door. "You can't tell us how to live!" she snarled. "It's our house, our yard, and our lives!"

For once, I was very calm. I told her, "If Phil wants to work here another day, you need to do what I'm asking you to do."

The next day, I told Phil, "Either get on the team, or y'all need to leave. It's that simple." He resigned, and they left town.

> *"The only thing more expensive than hiring a*
> *professional is hiring an amateur."*
> —Paul Neal "Red" Adair, oil well firefighter

THE MISTAKES KEPT COMING

That was an important educational experience for me. From then on, I was much more intentional and thorough in the hiring process. Even then, I made some truly boneheaded hires. I hired people who weren't qualified for jobs, and I put people in the wrong roles because I didn't understand their strengths. For instance, we hired Jessica Johnson as our media and marketing director. Let me just say that she didn't fit that role. She loves kids, so we moved her to be one of our three children's pastors, and she's a spark plug. She's wonderful working with kids and their parents. In most churches, it's a struggle to get people to volunteer in the kids' ministry, but Jessica has a gift for recruiting, training, placing, and encouraging an army of volunteers. She also leads worship a few times a year.

A creative director was recommended to me by a good friend who's also a pastor. We do some pretty big productions at Cornerstone, so I was glad to have someone with a lot of experience. As soon as he walked in the door, we planned a major production over several weeks, featuring major Bible characters. I told him to have a dress rehearsal on the Saturday before the first performance, but when I arrived, no one was in costume. I asked him why everyone wasn't ready for a complete run-through. He told me, "That's not how I do it."

The next morning, as the actors got ready and the service was about to start, I walked up to the guy who was playing Abraham. His beard was falling off, so I reached up, took the shreds off his face, and put them in my suit pocket. It was a "high school play gone bad"— completely unacceptable and not at all up to the standards we'd set.

Our new creative director made adjustments over the next two weeks, and things got better. But then, the fourth week—the finale— had Jesus on stage. Everything went well until the ascension at the end of the performance. The director could have rented a lift that swept up the actor above the curtains in a smooth, dramatic fashion, but to save money, he used a mechanical wench that jerked every six inches or so. Jesus made a not-too-graceful ascension into heaven, but it also was not quite far enough—his feet dangled beneath the curtain at the top of the stage, and we heard a muffled, "Help! Help!" Not exactly the risen Savior in glory.

Our new creative director knew what was coming. The day before, in the dress rehearsal, he'd resisted my input and told me, "Listen, you're going to have to learn to work with me. I'm in charge of this, and you're not."

I looked him in the eye and corrected him: "You don't get to work *with* me until I'm convinced you're working *for* me."

He said, "We'll talk about that on Monday."

And we did. But the outcome wasn't what he had anticipated. Monday, we agreed to go our separate ways.

> *"Nothing we do is more important than hiring people. At the end of the day, you bet on people, not strategies."*
> —Lawrence Bossidy

WHO MOVES?

One of my frustrations—perhaps my biggest one—was that I always expected people on our team to think like me, talk like me, and act like me. I'd hired them; it was my team, I was in authority as the pastor, and God had entrusted the church to me. It was each person's job, then, to do what I told them to do—to fulfill the agenda God had put on my heart. This expectation seemed reasonable to me, but it was, in reality, a deeply flawed leadership philosophy. I had to learn that it's not *either* let people be themselves *or* follow me; it's both-and. A team works most effectively when people operate within their gifts, are empowered to maximize their talents, and work together under the leadership of the pastor to accomplish more than they could do on their own. Yes, I know—this sounds like Leadership 101. But I had to take remedial courses before I was ready for that.

For too long, I expected people on my team to adjust to me; I learned that I need to adjust to *them*. Each person has a unique motivational style, unique talents, unique experiences, and unique dreams. When I understood this, I trained more specifically, placed more strategically, gave more room to some so they could fly, and supervised some more closely because they needed it. If I used a one-size-fits-all approach, I'd be right on target with some, a little off with most, and I'd completely miss the hearts of a few people. When I finally learned to hire with realistic expectations, I stopped imagining that every person would knock the ball out of the park as soon as they walked through our door. I spent more time getting to know them, finding the best fit for them, and making sure we were all focused on God's agenda.

When we look at Jesus' "hires," we see that He spent some time with three sets of people. Luke tells us about the 70 He sent out and welcomed back. We're more familiar with the 12 disciples who represented the 12 tribes of Israel. Among the 12, He had a special relationship with three: Peter, James, and John. He asked these three to join Him when He raised Jairus's daughter from the dead; on the Mount of Transfiguration, where they got a glimpse of His glory; and in the Garden of Gethsemane as He agonized in prayer. Jesus didn't stand up and make a plea for volunteers. He prayerfully put people where they belonged in His ministry and in His life.

As I explain in another part of this book, I met Gail in 1984 at Calvary Temple Church in Irving, Texas. I was serving as a custodian, and she was the church pianist. Before that day, our paths had been quite different: I'd been released from prison recently, and she'd graduated with a master's in piano performance. Our relationship started in a whirlwind, and we married just a few months later. I write this in 2020, when we've been married for 35 years and counting. We have four children and six incredible grandchildren. Gail has walked with me through every season and has always found a way to make a difference. For the 27 years I served as the Lead Pastor of Cornerstone, she lifted the music department to become a significant part of the church. She is wise beyond her years, gifted more than anyone I know, and insightful at a unique level. I appreciate her perspective today more than ever. To be honest, I wish I had listened to her more often, more intentionally, and sooner.

❧ • • • ❧

SOMETIMES, YOU CAN SEE A train wreck coming, but the derailment of an entire department isn't easy to watch—especially when the conductor didn't listen to the warnings. For me, the difficulty was that I couldn't warn the conductor … for a lot of reasons. I wasn't the head of the department. I was just an integral part of it.

For three decades, I've served our church in the creative department. Our church is located in a hub of the entertainment world: Nashville. At times, I was either running the entire department in interim or handling parts of it. How can there be weak hires in creative departments? It usually occurs when the creative pastor/manager/director, executive pastor, or worship pastor begins to actually *do* all the things they're supposed to *manage*. I often mused, *Don't they realize that we notice when they don't know their stuff? We're a church (and a city) full of pros.*

It was usually the case that our creative or worship pastor wasn't proficient in all aspects of music and production; but then, very few are. The smart ones staff to their weaknesses—like any smart leader. It's been my pleasure to add the missing gears and parts necessary to move the train down the track, so I've filled many of these leadership potholes. I did this for the sake of the people on the team (ours are all volunteers) and the support of the creative department leadership. I only wanted to make the leader successful.

God has equipped me for this role. I have degrees in performance and production with professional experience outside the church. I'm a music arranger for vocals and instrumental. I've assisted in directing, and I have directed. I have relationships with vendors for technical aspects in town—and I've maintained our church's reputation with those vendors. I'm saying all this simply to say that I've been in the trenches with our people—on the stage, under the stage, dripping with paint, with a drill in my hand, my foot on the sewing machine pedal, and at rehearsals poking and arranging parts based on the abilities and ranges of the performers. I think of myself as someone who's going to help people do their best and pursue excellence in performance and production, whether it be for a single worship service or for the most complex of events.

There is an imaginary line drawn of position and propriety in regard to *what* needs to be communicated to the conductor of the train and *who* should report it. It's not, and has never has been, me.

The conductor is my husband. Years ago, a wise saint under the anointing of the Holy Spirit delivered words to our church, and those words were, "KEEP RANK and keep marching." So I dutifully and cheerfully offer skills and respond to questions on guidance only when Maury asks for it ... this includes hiring staff members.

There are several contributing factors to hiring mistakes. The first and most important step is checking references; however, too often, that step was neglected. When a mistake is made, it often shows up quickly. It's hard to watch when you see significant problems within the first two weeks of someone's employment. I remember sitting in a rehearsal when a comment was made about a song lyric—a comment over a major point of conflict related to doctrine. I took note; sure enough, that hire was gone in less than a year, primarily over doctrinal disagreement ... not to mention the fact that he was more interested in self-promotion in the music industry than in the people who called our church home. Not returning calls, emails, or texts to our people showed his lack of interest.

Staffing your weaknesses can go too far when you exclusively hire out all the things that our people take so much pride in doing themselves. I remember an era when it was advised that a team of executives would manage the details on Maury's plate—departments such as media, music, and communication. A young man was hired as one of the executives to manage this arm of ministry—primarily, it seemed, based upon the fact that he said he worked closely with two very well-known pastors and leadership giants. He told us lots of stories about his connections. We later learned that he had a limited role with two organizations, and that he had absolutely no experience in all the things assigned to him at our church. It simply doesn't work to have team members give oversight to people and activities when they have no experience or expertise. When the people under him realized his incompetence, he issued a gag order to prevent them from telling Maury. This train was headed for a disaster!

I was in a difficult place. Even sharing a pillow didn't give me the right to speak up, so I kept quiet until I was asked. But if asked, I could speak from knowledge. Meanwhile, I just prayed to God that the heart of the king was in His hands (Proverbs 21:1). God knows, and He sees. This way, it's His will … not me manipulating the situation.

Without humility and the ability to properly delegate, some new hires see themselves as experts on every aspect of our team, all the way down to lighting people, camera operators, and set designers. It doesn't work to make last-minute changes. I vividly remember what I termed the "perilous periscope incident." We parked a Jeep on the stage for a Memorial Day service. The executive pastor over the creatives added something after a final dress rehearsal, which is a big no-no in our world because cameras had already set their shots and lighting was completely programmed. Moving a single prop or adding something can cause big problems that aren't easily corrected when the cameras roll a few hours later. This guy mounted the periscope on the Jeep dead center in front of the stage, but he didn't tell the camera operators. They had to switch all of their angles on the fly during the event … because the periscope appeared right at crotch-level on the speaker! (I wondered if we'd ever attract any more professionals for our team.)

No one is a perfect hire, but some people come with their own agendas, and some simply aren't qualified. There's always room for a leader to grow. I'm continually praying that God will enable us to take the people of the Kingdom to a higher level. At Cornerstone, we've hired some wonderful and gifted people, but we've also pulled the trigger too quickly and hired people who weren't a good fit … for any number of reasons. Through it all, God has worked—and for that, I'm glad.

MY ADVICE

I have a lot more advice about what *not* to do than advice about what to do, but let me communicate a few principles I'm learning.

1) **Trust, but verify.**

This was President Reagan's way of dealing with the Soviet Union as the relationship thawed and the USSR crumbled from within. It's a good thing to value people, love people, and believe the best of people; but the hiring process is your best and only real opportunity to do a complete background check. If you have to do it later, it's because you didn't do a good enough job earlier. Don't merely read referral letters and recommendations; call people to get behind-the-scenes information. During the interview, don't be afraid to ask hard questions. Listen for what's said, but also for what's not said. If a topic makes the person feel a little uncomfortable, pursue it; don't avoid it. And look at the employment history to see the track record of longevity. If a prospective staff member has moved every few years, that's at least a yellow flag, if not a red one. Of course, younger people don't have as much of a history, but carefully analyze where they've been and how they feel about their previous employers.

2) Listen to your wife.

Oh my. I wish I'd followed this advice far more often! Did I mention already that I'm not the most sensitive person in the world? And I'm not extremely perceptive when it comes to people. But Gail is. I thought I knew better because I'm on the ground every day in the life of the church, and I have the biggest investment in the new hires, but Gail often had far better insights about people than I did.

3) Listen to other perceptive people.

Most of us have people on our teams who see things we don't see and sense things we don't sense. My daughters and my brother are like that. For almost every person we've hired over the years, within two months, these individuals know whether that person is going to last on our team. They could have told me their observations much earlier … if only I'd asked. (I found out they made bets on how long certain people would be with us until I fired them or they left on their own.)

4) Hire to the role, but make sure there's a cultural fit.

I remember the Dallas Cowboys often drafted "the best athlete still on the table," and they'd find a position for those players. That may have worked for them, but that's not how we did things. We carefully analyzed the role we wanted to fill: youth pastor, children's pastor, marketing director, media director, worship leader, administrator, senior adult pastor, administrative assistant, day care director, and on and on. We crafted a detailed job description so we'd know what qualifications were needed to do the job well. But the culture of our church—and the nature of my leadership—is structured and disciplined. Some people chafe at this kind of leadership; I find it freeing because it provides direction and clarifies decisions. I need to know before people are hired if they can thrive in our culture.

5) **Know everyone's "leadership love language," and uncover it in the interview process.**

I remember a conversation with my executive pastor, Robby McGee. He told me, "You honor people the way you feel honored, but you don't understand what makes them feel honored. You thought giving them a paycheck was telling them, 'You're valuable. I'm glad you're here. When you don't get one, you'll know you're done here.' But that's not what inspires most people. They need more than that."

Disappointment is created by the gap between expectation and reality. For far too long, I was my own worst enemy because I didn't think I needed to do the hard work of conducting background checks, asking hard questions, and spending time getting to know people before I offered a position ... or didn't offer one. I could have saved myself a lot of worry.

CHAPTER 6

I WAS POLITICALLY DIVISIVE

"Let us not seek the Republican answer or the Democratic answer, but the right answer. Let us not seek to fix the blame for the past. Let us accept our own responsibility for the future."
—John F. Kennedy

I've studied the motives of the Spanish, French, Portuguese, and English explorers, as well as America's Founding Fathers. I'm convinced God had His hand on this country from the beginning. The diaries of Christopher Columbus describe how the Holy Spirit led him to find the New World and explore it on three expeditions. Over a century later, on Saturday, November 21, 1620, the Mayflower

Compact was signed on board before the Pilgrims set foot on land. Elder Brewster was asked to write it. In part, it reads:

> In the name of God, Amen. We whose names are underwritten, having undertaken—for the glory of God, and advancement of the Christian faith—a voyage to plant the first colony in the Northern parts of Virginia, do solemnly and mutually in the presence of God, and one another, covenant and combine ourselves together into a civil body politic, for our better ordering and preservation and furtherance of the ends aforesaid; and by virtue hereof to enact, constitute, and frame such just and equal laws, ordinances, acts, constitutions, and offices, from time to time, as shall be thought most meet and convenient for the general good of the colony, unto which we promise all due submission and obedience.[3]

Over the following few decades, more devout Christians sailed to Massachusetts Bay and settled in the region. Harvard University was founded in 1636. One of the founders explained the school's purpose:

> After God had carried us safely to New England, and we had built our houses, provided necessaries for our livelihood, reared convenient places for God's worship, and settled the civil government; one of the next things we longed for, and looked after was to advance learning, and perpetuate it to posterity; dreading to

---

3 "What was the Mayflower Compact? It's Meaning and Significance," Christianity.com, https://www. christianity.com/church/church-history/timeline/1601-1700/the-magnificent-mayflower-compact-11630074.html.

> leave an illiterate ministry to the churches, when our
> present ministers shall lie in the dust.[4]

Of the first 108 colleges founded in America, 106 had strong Christian origins and purposes. The letters and other papers of the colonists and the founders of the country contain countless expressions of deep faith in God and the desire to spread the gospel to everyone in the new lands. In fact, in the election of 1800, between the incumbent John Adams and his rival Thomas Jefferson, one of the widespread rumors against the challenger was that he was actually an atheist, and it almost cost him the election.

For 20 summers, I taught a course on the Christian foundations of our nation. One of the points I made was the common belief, in the first decades of our nation, that, if they didn't use Blackstone's Commentary and the Bible in law schools, the American legal system would lose its moorings.

When people hear me talk about the importance of moral absolutes, they assume I'm a card-carrying Republican. I'm not. I'm a card-carrying biblical absolutist. The Republican platform has many planks I agree with, but some that I don't. I've learned, from the Pilgrims and the faithful men and women who founded our nation, that the truth of God's Word is our ultimate standard—not a political party.

KEEPING FIRST THINGS FIRST

My beliefs have gotten me in trouble a number of times. I didn't have any hesitation telling our people not to vote for Al Gore, because

---

4 "Harvard's Founding," The Crimson, October 6, 1884, https://www.thecrimson.com/article/1884/10/6/harvards-founding-this-quaint-account-of/.

he supports abortion on demand. I told them to vote for George Bush. The Internal Revenue Service had a problem with my stand on the candidates—and they threatened to revoke our church's tax-free status. I have to admit that I went too far. My role as a pastor is first to save sinners—not to save America. But if we save America, we'll still be able to preach without government restrictions. I've had to back off of my hard-line political stance and focus on salvation. When people's hearts are right, they'll have godly values, and they'll stand up for God's purposes. When I told people how to vote, I was cutting corners on this process.

Over the years, elected officials and candidates from our area (and the state) have asked me to introduce them to our congregation—and they've asked for my support. I always review their voting record or campaign stands before I give anyone a thumbs up. If they have a history of voting for abortion, they won't get my support. I regularly told them, "When you're talking to our people, tell them the truth about what you believe and where you stand on the issues. If you don't, I'll talk about you on my television show." It wasn't an empty threat.

Sometimes, people ask me if I'm a "one-issue guy." If the issue is abortion, yes—I can live with that label, because it seems to me that the killing of innocents is very dear to the heart of God. I know that many women suffer from intense feelings of guilt for having abortions, and I see their contrition as a sign the Spirit of God is working in them to bring them to a point of repentance. God's forgiveness is high, wide, long, and deep, and it covers every sin. I ought to know.

I believe Christians have a place in the public sphere, but I often went too far in how I expressed this belief. My political stance has limited the outreach of the church. About half the people in our area won't come because we're perceived as anti-Democrat. The truth is that I love the people who are Democrats because God tells us to love everybody; I don't love many of their policies—and it seems that people who listen to me don't realize that I distinguish between people who are Democrats and their policies. They assume that, if I'm against the policies, I must necessarily be against the people. If Jesus could love the Pharisees, who despised Him and plotted to kill Him, surely I can love Democrats. But, to be honest, I can see why people have concluded that I hate them. My rhetoric has been fierce against their policies, and I've run people off who might have listened to the message of God's amazing love. My central calling has been derailed by a passion that's not focused on God's primary purpose.

Just after Paul met Jesus on the road to Damascus, God called him to be His "chosen instrument … to bear My name before the Gentiles" (Acts 9:15). In the rest of Luke's account of the early church, we see Paul being beaten time after time. On many of those occasions, it was the Jews who attacked him. Was it because he had strayed from his calling to the Gentiles? I think so. He knew what God had commanded him to do, but he couldn't help himself—he felt compelled to preach to the Jews, and it got him in big trouble. I can relate. I couldn't help myself either. I operated out of my self-generated passion, not my God-given purpose.

When I've demanded that people believe what I believe about political policies and candidates—and believe it as strongly as I do—I've bombed bridges instead of building them. And every person I offended told their family and friends that our church isn't for them.

The ripple effect of my dogmatic political stands has reached every corner of our community.

IT'S COMPLICATED

As you can probably tell, my solution isn't to switch sides. That's not going to happen; however, I need to find ways of communicating my convictions that don't involve being belligerent. I've tried to see everything as either/or—black or white—but it's not always that easy. Convictions can be crystal clear, but we have to apply them with wisdom and compassion. This principle relates to all of the hot-button issues today: immigration, healthcare, race relations, economic opportunity, and homosexuality, to name the ones that are often the most inflammatory.

At one point, our church planned to build some athletic fields, and we needed clearance from the city. A woman on the city council asked to see me, and she insisted we meet at a restaurant. She's a lesbian, and she brought three gay pastors. When we sat down, she asked, "Are the fields going to be available for everyone in the community, or only for people who believe like you do?"

Before I answered, I asked her, "Why didn't you want to meet at our church?"

She quickly answered, "Because gay people aren't safe in your church."

I thought for a few seconds. "I don't understand. We've never hurt anyone."

She had a ready answer: "No, but you don't support the gay community."

"So," I responded slowly, "you assume that, because we don't endorse a homosexual lifestyle, we're not safe. Is that right?"

She nodded. "Exactly." She then turned to the issue at hand: "What's your purpose for the fields?"

That one was easy: "We want to create a place where families and individuals can come to have a good time; hopefully, some of them will come to our church."

She asked, "Will you let the ladies' rugby team practice there?"

I asked her, "Is it a rugby team, or is it a gay rugby team?"

"The team plays in a lesbian league," she replied.

"Will their jerseys have any insignia that says it's a gay team?"

"What difference does that make?" she asked. "Are you going to limit who can use the fields?"

I explained, "Yes, we'll have limitations. We aren't going to allow alcohol for the players or the people watching them. If Budweiser offers to make an appearance with their Clydesdales, we'll tell them, 'Thanks, but no thanks.' We have a message, and we don't want anything to interfere with our message to the people who want to use the field. We're happy for your rugby team to use the field, but only if you don't have a message that violates ours."

She retorted, "So it'll be anti-gay."

"No," I corrected her. "But the real question is, why are gays anti-Christian? I agreed for the team to use our fields as long as they don't advertise a homosexual lifestyle."

This debate went on for about two hours. Then, one of the pastors said, "I talked to someone who came to your church for help but you wouldn't help her."

"Tell me more about that," I said.

"She needed help, and all your church gave her was a box of groceries."

"If she got groceries," I explained, "it's because someone in the church interviewed her, and she said she needed some food." I didn't think I had to connect all the dots. It seemed pretty clear that the accusation was unfounded.

Another pastor insisted, "You need to have me preach at your church, so we can show solidarity to the city."

I shook my head. "It's not my goal to show solidarity with you. I love you, I want the best for you, but we're not on the same team." I wanted to provide some context for my answer. One of the pastors was a Methodist. I turned to him and said, "You sprinkle when you baptize, and I immerse. We could sit here for the next two hours and talk about why we believe our position is the right one, and at the end of that time, neither of us would have changed his mind. It's the same with homosexuality. We've talked for two hours, and neither of us has changed his mind. I'm happy to go to lunch with all of you, and I'll gladly buy lunch for you, but my position won't change."

We then came back to where we began. The woman on the city council grimaced. "So you want to build those fields and let only the people on them that support your church and your message. Is that right?"

It was time to be clear. "The people of our church gave the money for the fields to advance the cause of the gospel and extend the reach of our church. The people who *gave the money* determine how the fields will be used. The people who *didn't give any money* can ask for permission to use the fields, but they can't dictate the terms. You have no skin in the game, so you have no place at the table. Our goal is to get kids and their families saved."

She asked, "You mean your brand of Christianity?"

"Exactly." We were finally getting somewhere.

TRUTH AND LOVE

"As fire tempers steel, so hardships can temper the human soul."
—Raja Arasa Ratnam

Underneath my hard exterior is a tender heart. I've learned that truth without love comes across as harsh and demanding, and love without truth is empty sentimentality. Blending truth and love is essential, and to communicate them well, we need to understand how the hearer interprets our words. Like everything else in my life, I've learned the hard way.

When the triplets were born, our tiny son, Galen, had to be rushed to the neonatal ICU for a breathing problem. The doctor wasn't encouraging. He told me, Gail's mother, and others who were with us that we needed to pray hard for our baby. Gail had a C-section, so it took her a while to recover from the anesthesia, but the nurses brought one of the girls in every hour or so to feed.

Gail's mother was freaking out. Her baby girl was facing the possibility of the greatest trauma any parent can suffer: the loss of a child. Gail's mother was sobbing. She told me she was going to tell Gail what was happening with Galen, but I looked at her and said sternly, "No, you're not going to tell her. It's not time. You need to get control of yourself. You've been a Christian all your life, and you're falling apart. You need to go to the hospital chapel and get right with God!"

That may have been truth, but it certainly wasn't love. I was scared to death. I didn't want my emotions to spiral out of control, so I wasn't willing for hers to be out of control, either.

With incredible insight, especially in that moment, my mother sent Billie Jean to pray. My mom looked at me and said, "Let me tell you something. I know your story, your home life, your history with military school, and crime. Your whole emotional formation happened from crisis to crisis. You got saved in prison. You've constantly lived in the fire. You've been tempered for this moment, but you need to give her room to feel what she feels about her daughter and her grandbabies. Not everyone is tempered in the fire."

Message received. When we empathize with people, we realize their strengths aren't our strengths, so their responses aren't how we respond, and their feelings may be quite different from ours. I'd failed to identify Gail's mom's feelings and have compassion for her before I opened my mouth. It was a big mistake. In the same way, I've often failed to empathize with the political views of people, so I gave them my truth with very little love. It wasn't that my truth was flawed, but they couldn't hear it because it wasn't tempered with compassion.

I believe that being created in the image of God means each of us has an inherent sense of justice. We don't have to teach children about it. From the time they can talk, they yell, "It's not fair!" When we think of justice, we can draw a hard line and refer only to punishing the guilty. It's certainly that, but in the Bible, God's justice is also caring for the poor. For instance, the psalmist writes, "I know that the

LORD will maintain the cause of the afflicted and justice for the poor" (Psalm 140:12). James gives us a glimpse of how God values both justice and righteousness: "Pure and undefiled religion in the sight of our God and Father is this: to visit orphans and widows in their distress, and to keep oneself unstained by the world" (James 1:27).

Generally, Republicans support small government and personal responsibility. If someone is hungry, he needs to get a job and make something of his life. Their personal progress involves making better choices, because many problems are self-inflicted. However, this perspective comes across as harsh and unloving to many who are disadvantaged. Democrats see government as the answer to the problems of the poor. They advocate caring for those in need, but they can be perceived as enabling and perpetuating poor habits.

Is it possible to be compassionate *and* ask people to be responsible? Yes—that's exactly how God relates to us. He knows the worst about us, but He loves us still, and He gives clear commands in the Scriptures about how we should live. His commands aren't designed to limit our freedom, but to eliminate the barriers to blessing. I believe Republicans, too often, aren't as compassionate as they should be, and Democrats don't insist on personal responsibility as much as people need them to do so. There's a third way ... God's way. I believe we can see all the major issues today—race, immigration, the drug crisis, healthcare, homelessness, fiscal and tax policy, gun control, climate, and the rest—through a gospel lens that combines genuine compassion with the need for personal responsibility. This approach may not generate simple answers, but the answers we find may actually work.

In our polarized political climate, we don't simply disagree with people on the other side—we consider them fools. Jesus engaged everybody, no matter their beliefs or their background. He was more than willing to spend time with anyone who would listen, and He poured out His love on the rich and the poor, the ultra-left Sadducees and the ultra-right Pharisees.

> *"Peace cannot be kept by force: it can only*
> *be achieved by understanding."*
> —Albert Einstein

I can't point any fingers at "those people" who inflame spite against those who disagree. I've been guilty of throwing gas on that fire far too often and for far too long. I am brought up short when I read Solomon's obviously true observation: "A gentle answer turns away wrath, but a harsh word stirs up anger" (Proverbs 15:1). And I wish I'd applied this advice from Solomon many years ago: "The words of the wise heard in quietness are better than the shouting of a ruler among fools" (Ecclesiastes 9:17).

Years ago, I was on PTL with Jim Bakker, and he had another guest, Jerry Falwell. I'd known Jerry for a number of years, and when he saw me from a distance, he yelled in his deep, booming voice, "Maury Davis!" He came over and told me, "You Pentecostals prophesy. I don't, but this is prophetic: You're like me. When somebody meets you, you make a quick decision—pucker up or duck! There's nothing in between." He was right about puckering up and fighting back, but he was wrong about ducking the conflict. I'm afraid I *relished* the conflict.

A few years ago, I preached a series on the truth about Islam. I interviewed a local imam so I would get the information straight from the source, in addition to reading a number of books on the subject. I talked about the origins in the seventh century, the conquest of the Near East and much of Europe, and the religion's influence in the world today. Sometime later, I was at a store when a lady walked up to me and said, "Pastor Maury, I miss our church so much!"

I asked, "Where have you been?"

She kind of shrugged and told me, "When you did that series about Islam, I was sure the church was going to be bombed, so my husband and I changed churches."

Galen grew up in my home and church and carries the DNA of both. For the first 18 years of his life, I was his father, preacher, and pastor. Even with that level of molding, generational changes within the same DNA discovered a way to express themselves. Galen's honor for the past is visible, but his perspective for the present is necessary.

❦ • • • ❦

WHEN I GREW UP, NASHVILLE was a family-friendly, conservative city. I'm sure there were different perspectives, but I certainly wasn't aware of anything close to the polarization we have today. My dad's political views fit right in. But as Nashville changed, he was increasingly out of step with the city's new diversity—in thought, choices, and political stands.

As a young man, I moved away for a number of years to take roles at churches in Texas and Arizona. I soon realized there were church members on both sides of the political divide. I heard some tell me, "I can't see how a Christian can be a Republican because they don't care for the poor." Others took me aside to warn me, "Democrats are for killing babies, so they're obviously not Christians." It became apparent that, if I took a stand on one side or the other, I was effectively eliminating half of the people in the community from hearing the gospel of grace and coming to know Jesus. The kingdom of God has a much higher value than a political party.

I came back to Cornerstone in 2010. When I invited people to come to our church, a number of them shook their heads and told me, "Yeah … no. I'm not coming. That's the big, white, right-wing, conservative church, and I'm not comfortable with that." Our church's reputation was based more on being Republican than following Jesus … more on being politically conservative than being devoted to God's kingdom.

As soon as I moved back, I wanted to lead our church in "serve days" to care for people in Madison—one of the boroughs of Nashville. When I went to the Chamber of Commerce to tell them our plans, a woman on the chamber's committee quickly let me know that she didn't trust our church one bit, because Dad had been so divisive in his political rhetoric. She told me, "I call him 'Mayor Maury' because he thinks he's in charge of everything in this town!" Dad wasn't subtle. He attended chamber meetings and demanded action on his projects. If they didn't vote according to his wishes, his language became even harsher. He said things like, "If you don't vote this way, you're ungodly!" Thankfully, the woman on the committee believed me when I assured her that we would shoulder all the expenses and bring out all the volunteers. And we did. She was impressed. Eventually, she came to Cornerstone.

She's not the only one who was offended by my father. I've had conversations with many people over the years who've told me, "I used to go to Cornerstone, but your dad was so politically partisan that I stopped going. I wanted to go to church to hear about Jesus, not to be told who to vote for."

Around the time I came back, Dad hired a research company to tell us why the church had stopped growing. They talked to people in the community, and reported that a large number of them would never attend because they didn't fit the narrow demographic—ethnically and politically—of our church. As soon as I heard this report, I made a commitment to change directions from the course my dad had followed. I wasn't going to be political. I was going to call people—all people—to Jesus.

My dad thought this was a big mistake. He told me I couldn't make an impact on the political leaders in the community if I didn't take a bold stand. But because I wasn't overtly partisan, liberal and conservative public officials invited me to the table to give input. I didn't use my pulpit to bully them into submission. Instead, I treated them with respect and communicated reasoned positions on issues important to our church and to the whole community. I didn't water down my faith in the least. In their board rooms, I was very candid about my beliefs—and they asked for my opinion on a wide range of topics. Doors were opened to me that had been closed to my dad.

In the early years of our country, pastors shaped the values of the nation and had a profound impact on the politics. Heart change was the source of morality and cultural change. Today, however, it seems we've gotten this backward. Many pastors seem to be more interested in their people's political persuasions than in their convictions about the love, wisdom, and power of God. Or, to put it another way, it appears that many conservatives are first Republicans and then Christians, and many liberals are Democrats first and Christians second. Their "brand" of being American is more important than the Great Commission. That's the idolatry of nationalism. When Jesus comes back, He's not going to ride on an elephant or a donkey. He'll be coming in the clouds, full of glory! When He returns, He's not going to decide which side is right and which is wrong. He's coming to reign over all.

I moved away from the patriotism of the pulpit to the kingdom of the pulpit. When people love Jesus with all their hearts, God will impart His perspective and His values to them, and they'll vote accordingly. The priority, then, is imparting the life-changing gospel and letting God provide people with wisdom about how to apply His truth to today's problems.

—*Galen Davis, Senior Pastor, Cornerstone Church, Nashville, Tennessee*

MY ADVICE

I'm not sorry for the convictions I've had about all kinds of policy issues, but I deeply regret the way I've communicated about them—at least most of the time. It has taken me a long time, but I've learned a few things.

1) **Don't let your calling become polluted by your political passion.**

   The fruit of our evangelism and discipleship can be limited by distractions when we dive too deeply into the political fray. Competing priorities produce problems.

2) **Speak to everyone on the political spectrum.**

   For years, I assumed everyone listening to me was as conservative as me. That was a strategic mistake. When we prepare messages, we need to think about the people we *want to be* in our audience, not just the ones who are *already there*. If we speak to people of different persuasions, they'll come.

3) **Watch your tone.**

   I said a lot of right things in the wrong way. If I'd taken more time to explain the whys behind what I believe, and if I'd lowered the decibel level, the people who were already with me would have still been with me, and I might have nudged the others a little closer to my views. The younger generation has a finely-tuned ear for our words and our tone. Many of us grew up in a time of segregation, but they don't see color the way most older people do. We grew up with few immigrants in our communities, but they feel completely comfortable with people from other lands. Today, fire-breathing pastors are attracting older people who want things to go back to the way they were 40 or 50 years ago, but they're not attracting many young, idealistic people, who want to know how Christians can possibly read the Bible and yet miss the message of love.

4) Don't tell people how to vote.

Boldly and clearly teach the biblical perspective on each issue, and let your people connect the dots. Trust them; they can do it. If we sound like we're running someone's campaign, we'll certainly alienate people that Jesus died to save. Stay in your lane as the pastor of your church.

I have no idea how many people would have come to faith in Christ, become disciples, and lived for God's kingdom if I hadn't been so divisive. Without exactly saying it, I drew a line in the sand and forced people to choose: for my political persuasions or against them. My passion for politics felt so right, but the damage I inflicted on people was so wrong. Please don't misunderstand—some people are ready to write me off as a liberal at this point!—I'm not suggesting we water down the truth to appeal to more people; but I made the colossal mistake of speaking the truth in a way that wasn't winsome or helpful. I ran off some people in the church, but the reputation I developed in the community kept far more people from even considering Cornerstone … and maybe even Christ. I have to live with that.

CHAPTER 7

I DIDN'T LISTEN TO ADVICE

*"Ears that do not listen to advice, accompany
the head when it is chopped off."*
—African Proverb

When I asked Sam Chand to be my coach and consultant, I had no idea how instrumental he would become in my life. Before Sam came onto the scene, our church had plateaued, and I was desperate to kick-start growth again. Instead of carefully thinking through any changes we needed to make in our culture and our team, I'd become impulsive, making changes fast and furiously. Some of them needed to be made; many didn't.

One of the new hires told me that Sunday school was past its time. We needed to get on the small group bandwagon "like all the other great and growing churches in the country. That's the future," he assured me. At the time, we had 1,700 in our adult Sunday school program. When we switched to small groups, we lost a lot of people—not just out of Sunday school, but out of the church. Many of them looked for other churches with good Sunday school programs. Abrupt change is hard on people, especially if it takes away something they treasure and replaces it with something they don't value. We didn't just create a wound that needed to be sewn up and healed; it was a full scale amputation.

I blew that one, and I blew it even more with that staff member. Quite often, when I asked him to do something, he was passive-aggressive. He said, "Sure, I'll get on it," but he didn't lift a finger to make it happen. When I told him not to change some things, he said, "No problem," and then changed them anyway. It wasn't long after he arrived that Pastor Sandy came to me and said, "He's going to give you a lot of headaches." She was wrong. My head was already throbbing.

A few weeks later, Sam came to one of our staff meetings on his first visit to Cornerstone. The independent-minded staff member had plenty to say, mostly because I directed every point to him to get his opinion. Why did I do that? That's a great question. I think it's because I wanted to placate him and get him on my side. Giving him an out-sized voice on the team was my attempt to lessen his negative impact. The staff meeting went on for over an hour, and this guy had more to say than all the other people put together. I saw Sam writing a note, and he passed it to me. It said, "If you keep feeding that chimpanzee, he'll turn into a gorilla!"

Point taken … but taken slowly. About a month later, I talked to Sam on the phone, and he asked, "Have you let him go yet?"

I tried to explain. "No. I need to, but I haven't yet."

Sam was insistent. "Why not?"

I don't know if he could hear me take a deep breath over the phone, but I told him, "Sam, I've fired and hired so many people in the last year that our team feels like they're on a merry-go-round. I'm pretty sure I've fired too many people, and I don't want to make the same mistake again." I needed our team to wear name tags each week to be sure all the new people knew our names. I'd become insecure and lacked confidence in my ability to make the right decisions. I wasn't listening to Sandy and Sam—the two people who saw things clearly. We'd had three youth pastors in the previous year, and that's just *one* position I'd changed multiple times. My fear of looking like a weak leader by firing one more person caused me to keep the one person I needed to fire more than all the rest.

Sandy had been with me for decades, and I'd benefited from her advice more times than I could count. Sam is one of the smartest, most perceptive people on the planet. I should have listened to both of them, but I was too insecure. It's odd. When I should have been most open to the advice of trustworthy people, I was defensive and indecisive, trusting in my own clouded opinion instead of their crystal-clear advice.

For my entire career, I'd been like a lion, stalking my next goal and using all my skills to reach it. But during this time, I was more like a squirrel on a busy street, scampering this way and that to dodge the tires that seemed to come from all directions at the same time. And I was about to be squashed.

> *"Listening to advice often accomplishes far more than heeding it."*
> —Malcolm Forbes

PLUGGED EARS

Gail doesn't give me advice unless she thinks I'm truly missing something. A few years ago, when we had worship leaders coming through our church doors as if it was a turnstile, a new leader was practicing with the band. Gail is a professional pianist, and she has been extremely involved with our music. That night, the drummer asked our worship leader, "You don't give us any hand signals. How will we know when to change to the next song?"

He said, "I don't do it like other worship leaders. I want you to keep your eyes on my butt the whole time, and when I wiggle it, you'll know what to do."

Gail came home and told me about the directions given to the band. She said, "Maury, you've got a problem. The guys in the band aren't going to stick around if that's the kind of leader they have. That's the craziest thing I've ever heard!"

I didn't pay attention to her—and, to her credit, she didn't nag me at all. A few weeks later, a couple of guys in the band asked to see me. I wondered if it had anything to do with the rear end of the worship leader. One of them told me, "Pastor, we've been in the band for a long time, but we're done. We're not going to be in his band."

I asked, "Do other people in the band feel the same way?"

"Yes, they do," came the reply.

I was looking at a musical revolt. I had a choice: fire the worship leader or lose the church members. It was an easy decision: One costs money, and the other gives money.

> *"Only the wisest and the stupidest of men never change."*
> —Confucius

A WEALTH OF WISDOM

Thankfully, God has put some very wise people in my life:

Gail is a terrific source of insight into people and situations. She knows me, and she knows when people are responding positively to my leadership.

In marketing, my daughter Danielle is a genius. I always go to her for direction regarding publications and media.

My daughter Gabrielle is a brilliant accountant. If I need input about finances, she's my go-to resource.

Pastor Sandy has been with me for decades, and we've gone through all kinds of battles together. She has a perspective that's both broad and long—she understands every ministry in the church, and she's seen the ups and downs over the long haul.

Pastor Deanna is very discerning. She compassionately and effectively pastors an enormous number of people in the church.

Robby McGee was my executive pastor and is now a business coach and consultant. I've often called him and said, "Hey, I've got this problem. Let me run it past you and see what you think I should do."

Pastor George was my father figure from the time I was in prison to when he passed away, and I asked him for advice about every significant choice in my life.

Ron McManus and Sam Chand have given me the incredibly valuable perspective of experts from the outside who can see what I couldn't see.

All of these people have their own unique talents, gifts, and perceptions, and I trust them to be completely honest with me. Solomon had a wealth of wisdom (except when it came to women). He wrote, "Faithful are the wounds of a friend, but deceitful are the kisses of an enemy" (Proverbs 27:6). Over the years, I've learned—the hard way, most of the time—that it's not smart to listen only to people who tell me what I want to hear.

The Harvard Business review recently told a story about Cees 't Hart, CEO of the Carlsberg Group. When he was first hired, Mr. Hart was given private access to an elevator to his penthouse office. It didn't take long for him to feel isolated. After a couple of months, he moved himself to a desk in an open floor plan out among the people. He said, "If I don't meet people, I won't get to know what they think. And if I don't have a finger on the pulse of the organization, I can't lead effectively." If I'd had my finger on the pulse of my congregation, I wouldn't have canceled Sunday School like I did. I wouldn't have made some of those hiring decisions. I was in a place fed by people who didn't have the church's best interests at heart, but instead only cared about their own jobs. In that same article, "Ego is the Enemy of Good Leadership," Ramus Hougaard and Jacqueline Carter conclude:

> As we rise in the ranks, we acquire more power. And with that, people are more likely to want to please us by listening more attentively, agreeing more, and laughing at our jokes. All of these tickle the ego. And when the ego is tickled, it grows … [A] big ego makes us have a strong confirmation bias. Because of this, we lose perspective and end up in a leadership bubble where we only see and hear what we want to. As a result, we lose touch with the people we lead, the culture we are a part of, and ultimately our clients and stakeholders.[5]

I was stuck in a leadership bubble I was trying too hard to break out of. It didn't take me long to figure out who was there to stroke my ego and who was there to get to the goal. The people who really love me are willing to face my defensiveness and excuses and still wade in to tell me the truth. Their observations may hurt, and their advice might cost me a lot, but these are my true friends.

I came to know Mark Quattrochi when I met him and his wife at Cornerstone. Mark reminded me of hippies from the 70s, with his long hair and humorous personality. Hiring him was a step of faith, but Mark's acquisition of space for a TV show on Channel 5 put Cornerstone at the center of Nashville's attention.

---

5   Rasmus Hougaard and Jacqueline Carter. "Ego is the Enemy of Good Leadership." *The Harvard Business Review.* Published November 06, 2018. https://hbr.org/2018/11/ego-is-the-enemy-of-good-leadership.

❧ • • • ☙

BEING ON PASTOR MAURY'S STAFF team at Cornerstone was both toxic and intoxicating. It was very unhealthy, but incredible things were happening in the ministry.

Before I joined the team, my wife had been attending Cornerstone for a long time, while I was often on the road. I worked in the music business as a performer, writer, and producer. Pastor Maury asked me to join the team to "make everything about our media better." I was thrilled! It sounded like the perfect job. He was asking me to bring my best talents to the team, and I felt excited to invest every ounce of my creativity and drive there.

My enthusiasm didn't last long. Pastor Maury is a strong leader, and I discovered that he's not usually open to new ideas. As a creative person, I was always thinking of ways to make things better. That's what he hired me to do, but that's not what he actually wanted. When people on the team offered new methodologies and talked about creative things other churches were doing, Pastor Maury listened for a few minutes and then squashed the idea in no uncertain terms: "We're not doing that!" Then he moved on. No more discussion, no useful application, no openness to ideas at all. For instance, as the student culture changed and our student pastor learned concepts from his peers in other churches, the new ideas he pitched at meetings were instantly shot down.

We realized we had to sell our ideas like we were used car salesmen—anything to make a deal. It wasn't enough to think carefully about the concept; we also had to think carefully about how we presented it to Pastor Maury. We were sure he'd oppose anything and everything, and we had to be strong enough to go toe to toe with him.

This kind of environment deflates enthusiasm and kills creativity. Who wants to have a fight over every idea? One by one, we learned that it wasn't worth it to try to change his mind, so we only presented ideas we knew he'd like—ideas we'd heard him talk about already. For those who had always worked in churches, it was hard. For me, someone who had lived on the creative edge my entire life, it was excruciating. In my world, the best ideas won the day, but in Pastor Maury's world, *his* ideas won every day. I simply stopped bringing any ideas. I became passive because I didn't want to be rejected every time, so I waited for Maury to bring his ideas to me. We had a lot of wonderfully gifted, creative people on the team, but our ceiling was Pastor Maury's creativity—not ours.

The environment was so bad that we had signals to use with each other when Pastor Maury pulled into the parking lot. We scattered to stay out of his line of fire. We knew that, when he walked in and found one of us, he'd ask a question—a loaded question. If he didn't get the answer he wanted, he might say, "You need to find another job!" It was completely over-the-top. I had no experience with people who treated me like that, so I often pushed back. There were times we stood face to face yelling at each other. It was much more stressful than anything I'd known in the music business.

Before I came on the staff team, Pastor Maury had meant the world to me. He had been the spiritual mentor for my wife and me, and our children had been dedicated at Cornerstone. We were spiritually fed and led there. We were all in. But soon after I joined the team, my frustration turned to anger, and that anger was reinforced every day. I stayed for a while, but it was obvious that it wasn't a good place for me. It was just too hard, too toxic, too limiting. I packed my things and left.

I've always had regrets—not about leaving, but about what might have been. Pastor Maury had plenty of vision. God consistently used his amazing testimony. One day, he asked me, "How can we use my testimony in a bigger way to bring people to Christ?" I suggested he start a television program. I put the wheels in motion, and we launched what still is one of the most popular broadcasts in the Nashville market, religious or secular. I often wonder, "Man, what could that show have become?" At first, it seemed to be a match made in heaven. Pastor Maury has an incredible testimony, he's a terrific communicator, and people in the community need Jesus. I could have used my experience and my skills to advance the church's message, but I wasn't allowed to do that.

I've been back to Cornerstone a number of times. Pastor Maury has invited me to leadership roundtables, and we still keep in touch. He's changed. I can see it in his face and hear it in his voice. It's hard to describe … weird, in fact. I actually asked someone, "Is this the same guy?" He's always been an excellent communicator, but now he is much more poised and positive. In fact, his voice now communicates care, respect, and an authentic interest in helping me and others. I leave our times together shaking my head and smiling, saying to myself, *This is the kind of leader I wanted to work for years ago.*

—*Mark Quattrochi, Lead Pastor, The Chapel*
Community Church, Tampa, Florida

❧ • • • ❧

MY ADVICE

I wish I'd learned the lessons about valuing advice much earlier in my life and in my career as a pastor. I'd tell other pastors …

1) **Learn to collaborate early and often.**

I was a top-down, my-way-or-the-highway leader. I was sure I knew what was best for the church, and I believed my God-given authority meant that I had to make all the decisions. My micromanagement prevented people from sharing all their ideas. We could have grown more if I'd valued their input.

2) **Practice active listening.**

People communicate powerful messages, but not always with their words. Of course, words are our primary means of communication, and as we listen, we look for meaning. The way I know I'm listening is when I ask second and third follow-up questions instead of jumping in to give my definitive opinion. I'm learning to notice a person's body language: closed or open, defensive or engaging, angry or compliant. When their posture and their words give conflicting messages, I need to slow down and find out what's really going on. And when I think I understand, I can say, "Let me tell you what I hear you saying," and explain the point as clearly as I can. This gives the person an opportunity to clarify anything I missed so he knows that I get it.

3) See the value in others.

This is an easy step for some leaders; it's in their personal and organizational DNA. But for some of us, it's a stretch. When people know we value them, they give their best. Isn't that what we want? A pastor asked me to help him get through a rough patch in his church's life. It didn't take long to figure out that his leadership style looked very familiar: He was authoritarian and micromanaged his staff. I told him, "Why don't you ask the people on your team to come up with the theme for next year?"

He reacted, "I've never done that!"

"I know," I assured him. "But it would motivate them if they felt they were part of the process of determining the emphasis of the church for next year."

He looked like I was asking him to give them the keys to the kingdom. I was. I explained, "Ask each of them to come up with three concepts that would inspire every person in the church—from children to seniors, on Sunday morning and in classes and groups. In the next staff meeting, write all of them on a whiteboard. Then, ask each one to vote so you can come up with the top five. Have them vote again to come up with the top three. When you have those, ask, 'Which of these will have the greatest impact and will motivate people in your area of ministry?' Unless it's entirely off the wall—which it won't be— go with it."

He asked, "Maury, why in the world would I do that?"

"Because—" I was stating the obvious, but it obviously needed to be stated—"you're showing that you value their advice ... and that matters to them. You're letting them participate in your level of leadership. They'll be more motivated than ever. This is just one way to build a collaborative team."

4) **Create a reconciling environment.**

When people don't feel heard, they get their feelings hurt, and they do things to either get attention or to put other people down. For many years, I didn't address "the elephant in the room"—our staff members' overt defiance or covert undermining of others with sarcasm. I just let it simmer ... and sour. But no longer. I'm committed to resolving disputes with honesty, forgiveness, and a process to rebuild trust. A man on our team told Sam Chand that he was the only professional on our staff. When I found out, I called our team together, and I said to him, "I heard that you told Sam Chand you're the only professional around here. You're demeaning the people on our team. Before you came, you'd never been on a church staff team. These people have built a great church, and they deserve your respect. I'm going to leave the room, and you need to reconcile with them. When I come back, it'll be up to them if you have a job at Cornerstone or not."

It's not entirely accurate that I didn't listen to advice, but I often made one of two errors: I listened to the wrong advice, or I didn't listen to good advice. None of us has a perfect track record of fil-tering out the bad and keeping the good, but my consistent inse-curity, punctuated by moments of frenzy, made me susceptible to too many bad choices regarding others' advice.

CHAPTER 8

I DIDN'T CELEBRATE OTHERS' WINS

"Celebrate the success of others. High tide floats all ships."
—Susan Elizabeth Phillips

One day, in a staff meeting, I put the agenda aside and asked, "How are y'all doing? How do you feel about being part of what's going on here at Cornerstone?"

In different ways, a number of people said they were "fine." Some reported that they were frustrated because of this or that. Then, I asked, "What's the number one thing you'd like to see us change that would make you happier in doing your job?"

One of the young men took a deep breath and said, "Pastor, sometimes I don't feel appreciated."

I'm not sure he was expecting my response. I asked, "Son, did you get paid last month?"

He stammered, "Yes. Yes, I did."

I hit him with my truth: "Every time I get a check, I feel totally appreciated." I let that sink in for a second or two. "If I need to walk around every day and pat you on the back, I'd rather find somebody who doesn't need that from me."

He shot back, "Pastor, it's not all about money."

"You're not married." I was sure that had nailed him. "When you get married and have kids, you'll know how important it is to get a regular paycheck." I turned to the rest of the team and then looked back at him: "We don't go to work for relationships, we don't go to work to raise our self-esteem, and we don't go to work to find a spouse. We go to work each day to make money." I paused for a second, and then closed the loop: "We go *to church* to make friends, we go *to church* to make a difference, we go *to church* to look for a spouse, and we go *to church* to participate in a community of like-minded believers. When we sit together in our staff meeting, this is the business side of life. We go to work to make money, and every time you get a paycheck, it says you're valuable enough to stick around until the next payday. When you get paid, it means you're still on the team, and it means I'm glad you're still on the team. That's how I show appreciation. The first time you don't get a paycheck, you can see it as a clear message that I'm not celebrating your accomplishments, and I'm no longer thrilled you're on the team. Got it?"

I'm sure most of the people in the room were shocked, but I considered it one of the best impromptu sermons I'd ever given.

People who'd been with me for a long time rolled their eyes. Pastor Sandy muttered just loud enough for everybody to hear, "There he goes again."

MY VERSION OF THE GOLDEN RULE

It may sound like I have no heart to celebrate people who've made a big difference in our church, but that's not true. The problem is that my efforts are often off-target. When our last building program was completed, I offered to take Dana Lawson and his wife to Kenya to thank him for his great work overseeing the entire process. It was, I was convinced, "the trip of a lifetime." When I told them about my plans, Dana told me, "I really appreciate it, Pastor, but my wife and I would much rather go to Hawaii."

I was surprised. "Really? Hawaii? But I want to honor you."

He said, "We've been going to Kenya for the past ten years. We've built 2,000 churches and provided water for hundreds of villages. We've been to Kenya, but we've never been to Hawaii."

I was offering to do for him what *I* wanted someone to do for *me*. It's my version of the Golden Rule, and it has severe limitations. In fact, I have a long and storied history of doing things to appreciate people that they didn't want me to do for them. My expressions of thanks were meaningful to me, but not to them. I was projecting my dreams onto them, and I had no consideration for their dreams.

I planned to take Gail to Hawaii for our 30th anniversary. I knew Sam Chand had just come back from Hawaii, so I called to ask his recommendation for a hotel and resort. He asked, "Maury, why are you asking?"

I told him I wanted to do something special for Gail on our anniversary. He told me about a hotel; then, the next day, he called me back and asked, "Have you ever been to Hawaii?"

"Yes," I explained. "I've been there before. It's spectacular. That's why I want to go again."

Sam said, "Maury, I've gotten to spend some time with you and Gail over the past year. In all of these conversations, I've never heard her mention a desire to go to Hawaii, but she has said several times that her dream is to go to Paris. If you really want to do something special for her, take her to Paris. After all, anniversaries aren't for the husband; they're for the wife." I didn't say anything for a few seconds, so he decided to continue. "Instead of going to a place where you can snorkel and surf and do the things you want to do, go to Paris where she can go to the finest museums and walk the beautiful streets of the city. I know you're a Marriott member. I've called the Marriott near the Eiffel Tower, and they have rooms on the dates you've planned for your trip."

A few weeks later, Gail and I were in the Louvre in the heart of Paris. Gail felt like she had died and gone to glory. I spent the day looking at her looking at paintings, sculptures, tapestries, and crown jewels. I'm a ten-second guy, with gusts up to 15. That's the entirety of my attention span for any artwork. I couldn't even force myself for the full ten when we got into the room with the Mona Lisa. It's just a dingy little painting of someone nobody can identify.

Needless to say, Gail spent a lot longer studying each piece. At one point, two ladies joined her as she looked at every detail of a painting. One of them wondered out loud why the paint looked different on the one they were standing in front of than the one next to it. Gail launched into an explanation of the way paint was mixed in different centuries. She was giving them scientific, historical, and cultural reasons why one paint was different from another. I was amazed—not because I was fascinated with the information, but because I had no idea anyone could possibly be interested in these details. I had no idea Gail knew all that, and I couldn't fathom why she even cared. All the painters had been dead for centuries. The only thing that mattered to me was where I could find some good old American food for lunch.

When we went to the Notre Dame Cathedral, she knew that the building was begun in 1163 and took centuries to complete. While she was examining the Gothic architecture, I took dozens of pictures of people posing with a guy dressed like the Hunchback of Notre Dame and posting them. Gail told me, "You're here at one of the wonders of the world, but you're taking pictures of a clown!"

I wanted to say, "So? What's your point?" but I decided to keep my thoughts to myself.

We finished our tour of the cathedral, and Gail asked, "Well, what do you think of this gorgeous place?"

My answer probably wasn't one shared by many other tourists: "That's what happens when you put a building program in the hands of creatives. They build a museum, not a church."

There was no snorkeling in the river that runs through Paris, and certainly no surfing anywhere near there, no hiking trails and no mountains to climb. I love to get outside and be active, but the only thing to do outdoors was to walk to the next museum or cathedral. My greatest pleasure was seeing how happy Gail was during the entire trip. At the airport, as we were about to fly back, she turned to me and said, "That was so much fun! Wouldn't you like to do this again?"

I wanted to say, "No! Never again!" Instead, I told her, "If that's what you'd like, dear, count me in."

ASSUMPTIONS

My experience with Pastor George powerfully shaped my identity, my values, and my expectations. He regularly came to see me when I was in prison. When he gave me a job after I got out, he invited me to be his shadow. I went almost everywhere he went and saw him in every conceivable situation. I went jogging with him every morning. I visited people in the hospital with him and saw him care for the sick. I drove him to out-of-town funerals, and I watched him handle problems and opportunities all day, every day. It was the highest honor just to be by his side. If he asked me to go somewhere with him, I rearranged my schedule. When I became a pastor, I assumed people on my team would consider it just as much of an honor to be with me. Over the years, I've learned that very few staff members view their pastor the way I viewed Pastor George.

On the day when Pastor George went to be with the Lord, I grieved as much as I did for my mother. He meant that much to me. He believed in me when no one else did. When he found me, I wasn't just tarnished—I was in the cesspool of crime and punishment. His love and faith in my future lifted me out of the mire and gave me hope that God might do something with me after all. It's not an exaggeration to say that all of the opportunities I've had have come because of Pastor George. However, it was misguided of me to assume that people who joined our staff team would feel the same way about me. I didn't find them when they were lost and hopeless, I didn't pursue a relationship with them when they had nothing to offer, and I didn't treat them like sons and daughters when others considered them unclean and unworthy—because, compared to me, they've never been unclean or unworthy. I wasn't involved in every aspect of their spiritual and leadership formation, so I didn't earn the respect, love, and loyalty from them that I had for Pastor George.

My assumptions may have been understandable from one point of view, but they were completely unrealistic and flawed. I was oblivious to my team's need for affirmation as valuable people, and their need for encouragement for their hard work and accomplishments.

A friend asked me if I treated my children the way I treated my staff team: by making wrong assumptions about the affirmation they needed. I'm afraid it was pretty similar. I didn't take cues from my kids about what was important to them. If Danielle celebrated because she won a spelling bee in her class, I wasn't impressed. I wanted her to reach her potential and be the champion of the entire school. Gabrielle was a brilliant student, graduating as valedictorian from Belmont University with a master's degree and the highest grade point average in the school's history. Danielle could have been first in her class, but she devoted much of her senior year to being the editor of the yearbook. Galen is very smart, but he was more interested in building friendships than raising his GPA. I didn't applaud him for spending time with people, because he was going to do that no matter what I required of him. I focused on his grades. When he was in the seventh grade, he made a C, and I grounded him for six weeks. I took him to a bookstore and told him to pick out 10 books. I didn't care what they were. For the next six weeks, Monday through Friday, he read those books. No radio, no television, no phone calls with friends … just homework and reading. Actually, during this time, Galen learned the value of reading, and those six weeks changed his life.

A PAYCHECK

> *"Be an encourager. The world has enough critics."*
> —Unknown

I think you could say I created an affirmation Sahara—dry, barren, and broad. Actress Celeste Holm accurately observed, "We live by encouragement and die without it—slowly, sadly, and angrily." The responses of people on our team were widely varied. Some redoubled their efforts to please me, with hope that they'd get a word of encouragement; some seemed to emotionally wither and die. A few people are so emotionally healthy and strong that they don't need much encouragement, but far more are emotionally fragile and spiral down into despair if they don't get consistent reinforcement. I saw this as a character flaw. It's not. It's just part of the human condition.

It wasn't that I thought encouragement was unimportant; it's that I thought what I was giving them was plenty of it. If I wasn't chewing on them, they should conclude they were doing a good job. And if they got a paycheck, that should be a loud and clear message that I believed in them. I was completely blind to the normal human need for consistent verbal support.

To show how my view is so different from everyone else, here's a glimpse into my mind: When I was on the staff team at Calvary, one day, Pastor George was very unhappy with something I'd done (or not done). He always used staff meetings to give direction to individual staff members, but this was more than direction. For about five minutes, he described my failings in great detail and with plenty of emotion. When he was finished, he must have thought I wasn't paying attention, because he growled, "Davis, are you getting this, or do I need to repeat myself?"

I responded, "I just want you to get it out of your system. Get it all out now. If you have more, let's hear it, and we'll be done with it."

That didn't sit very well with him.

Later, as I was having lunch with others on the team, one of them asked me, "Man, how do you feel when he chews on you like that? When he does that to me, I'm humiliated."

I explained, "You and I are coming from very different places. I was in prison working in a cotton field when a guard on horseback screamed profanities at me for working too slowly. I learned not to take it personally. I didn't want to have a heatstroke, so I wasn't going to speed up. I just said, 'Yes, boss,' and kept going at my same pace. That prison guard didn't care about me at all, but I was sure Pastor George loved me. If I can take it from a prison guard, I can certainly take it from someone who has been incredibly kind and supportive to me. Yes, he wasn't happy, but he still loves me. He's just having a bad day. It's no big deal."

"Celebrate what God has given others.
Leverage what God has given you."
—Andy Stanley

THE DAY THE LIGHTS CAME ON

I wish I could tell you that I learned the importance of affirmation early in my career as a pastor, but that wouldn't be the truth. Actually, the revelation came about six months after I'd moved out and my son Galen had become the pastor at Cornerstone. One day, I was in the office, and I casually asked Tammy, my administrative assistant, "How are things going?"

I was expecting her to say, "Oh, we sure miss you around here, Pastor Maury. Things just aren't the same." But she didn't say that. The second part of her statement was true, but not in the way I expected. She told me, "Since I've been here, the staff morale has never been this good!"

I felt a dagger stab me in the heart. I considered myself a high-level leader—a success at building a megachurch—a pastor who had built something great; but my son, a rookie, had created an environment on the staff team that was far more supportive than my 30 years leading the team. I had wiped this kid's rear end, but he was leaving me in the dust.

I told myself Tammy must be the only one who felt that way. Surely hers was an isolated opinion. I walked down the hall to talk to Sandy and a couple of others who had been around for quite a while, and told them what Tammy had said. I didn't dispute her report. Instead, I asked, "How could this happen so quickly?"

Sandy jumped to answer. "Because your son is incredibly encouraging."

I asked, "Okay, but what about me?"

Silence. Then another person gave a wry smile and said, "Mmmmm, not so much."

Sandy explained, "You have the spiritual gift of correction, not encouragement."

How much do people need us to encourage them? I'm reminded of the old story in which someone tells a man that he isn't saying, "I love you" enough to his wife. He replies, "I told her 'I love you' when I married her. When that changes, I'll be sure to let her know." That's basically how I led people for many years. The writer to the Hebrews tells us, "But encourage one another day after day, as long as it is still called 'Today,' so that none of you will be hardened by the deceitfulness of sin" (Hebrews 3:13). Throughout the Bible, we find references to "the day of the Lord" or "that day"—when Jesus returns and makes all things right. In this passage, however, the writer isn't pointing to the future; he's putting his finger on the present—right now, today. He says that we all need pointed, heart-felt encouragement to know, love, and follow Jesus. Without it, we forget what's most important; we spend our energies on being noticed instead of on honoring the One who already notices us. We jockey for position and power instead of being secure, humble servants like the One who was humble enough to die in our place. We need people to speak into our lives to affirm us in our devotion to Christ and His cause, and that's the same role we play in the lives of the people close to us. Every day.

I met Robby McGee when he was traveling with MidSouth as a songwriter. He was a Dove-winning, Grammy-nominated personality in our church. I invited him to come on staff as our Chief Financial Officer. Robby not only lifted a heavy load, but he was also responsible for creating systems and processes that still exist today. He's a man I trust and whom I'm grateful to know.

🎜 • • • 🎜

IN MORE THAN 20 YEARS of working with Pastor Maury, I've had plenty of opportunities to watch how he relates to people on his staff team. His record of celebrating others' success is checkered—sometimes good, sometimes bad. I think there were a couple issues that created the chasm between the two. He chose to honor and celebrate people in a way that he was comfortable with, or in a way he believed would convey honor, instead of in the ways that made each person feel honored.

On a trip to New Mexico to honor our board of directors and their spouses, Pastor Davis thought everyone would enjoy our version of an episode of "The Amazing Race." We got up early, grabbed a coffee to go, drove by all of the sites, stayed in our cars all day (secluded from the rest of the group), and rarely stopped—except to eat at his favorite spots. We packed as many miles as possible into every day. All of this perfectly suited his personality! However, it wasn't what people were expecting. They thought it was going to be a time of relaxation, sleeping in, drinking coffee, and stopping along the way to take pictures and enjoy the sites. By the end of the trip, he was amazed (and frustrated) that there were some who seemed unappreciative of the appreciation he had shown them for their service!

The second thing I noticed was that Maury didn't see the value in people's talents and spiritual gifts that happened to be significantly different from his; therefore, he didn't see these talents as something to be honored and celebrated. If you were extremely relational but unstructured, or a processor who was analytical and slower to move, you weren't as likely to get placed into the "honor and celebration" column. Although he and I had a great relationship, and though he definitely honored me throughout the years, there were times I frustrated him because I had the propensity to analyze things and move at a slower pace.

On one of these occasions, a projector was taken out of the sanctuary because it wasn't functioning properly. I had it repaired, but within a few days, it went out again ... right before one of our Friday morning prayer meetings! Maury and I met before the meeting, he realized the projector wasn't there, and he began to convey—in no uncertain terms—the way he felt about the projector not working—and, more to the point, my lack of concern that it wasn't working. I told him that, just because I didn't lose my temper, yell, and jump up and down didn't mean that I didn't care (implying, of course, that he was out of control). At that point, he left the room (Actually, he left the church property.) and left us with the awkward task of explaining his absence to the people who had come that morning to pray.

But Maury could certainly show honor to whom honor was due. When he first came to Nashville, he met a lady named Alice Jane

Blythe. She told him that, wherever he went, she was going to help him build a great church. A few years after he became the Lead Pastor at Cornerstone, he decided to hire Sister Blythe onto the staff, and he committed to pay her for as long as she lived. (She was in her seventies at the time.) He honored her for all her years of service in the ministry, and he continued to honor her throughout her twilight years. In all fairness, I don't think he had any idea she would live to be 101, but I'm confident that wouldn't have changed a thing!

—*Robby McGee, President of McGee, Inc., Dallas, Texas*

MY ADVICE

There's no telling how many opportunities I missed over the years to encourage people and to celebrate their contributions to our church and the kingdom of God. I started really late, and it's a steep learning curve, but I'm making progress. As they say, "Better late than never."

1) Be intentional.

Galen's ability to encourage others comes naturally, but I have to work at it. I'm learning to notice what people do well and to speak words of gratitude that let them know I appreciate them. I've discovered it's really not that hard, and it makes a difference. When I say, "Hey, what you did really made a difference in those people's lives," I see their eyes light up.

2) Become a Geiger counter of value.

When I'm around people who are having a positive impact on others, my internal "Geiger counter" needs to be activated so that it alerts me. For years, I measured value by only two metrics: money in the plate and posteriors in the pews. Now I'm learning to see value in the intangibles: kindness, tenacity, faithfulness, and love. When I notice these positive traits, I speak up to name and nurture them.

3) Know your people's buttons.

Identify their love languages. Some people feel affirmed when we talk about their character, others about their achievement, and still others about their commitment to a cause. Some are motivated by public applause; others prefer private acknowledgement. A *good* leader gives similar affirmation to everybody, but a *great* leader recognizes the specific encouragement that hits the motivational target in each person—staff member, spouse, kids, friends, and everybody in their inner circle of relationships. This commitment requires us to acknowledge how we're different from those around us. My leadership love language is numbers—if our congregation grows, I feel loved; if it shrinks, I feel like a colossal failure. Almost nobody is like me. Their love language might be a hug, kind words, a small gift, or time together.

4) Ask and listen.

Don't assume you know how to celebrate people in the most meaningful ways to them. Ask what will make them feel honored, listen, and change your plans to suit their wants. Send them to Hawaii instead of Kenya. Take them to Paris instead of Hawaii.

5) Give thanks.

Expressing gratitude is the easiest and most effective way to celebrate the people around us. If this isn't natural for you, spend time thinking of all the people who've contributed to where you are now, and realize that you have the God-given opportunity to contribute to the present and future of every person on your team. In *Leadership Is an Art*, Max DePree observes, "The first responsibility of a leader is to define reality. The last is to say thank you. In between, the leader must become a servant and a debtor."[6] A debtor? Yes—we're indebted to the people who have forsaken comfort, wealth, and status to follow Jesus and to join us in building His church. They deserve our thanks.

What took me so long? I can think of all kinds of reasons and excuses, but at this point, none of them matter. What matters is how I treat people *today*—the impact I make on their hearts as well as their performance. Celebrating people isn't optional equipment for leaders; it needs to be standard on every model.

I'm grateful for people who loved me and had the courage to tell me the truth about how far I'd missed the mark in affirming those around me. I've learned from them, and the Spirit of God is working to change me from the inside out. For the rest of my life, I want to be more like Jesus and pour love into the lives of others ... but I'd settle for being a lot more like Galen.

---

6   Max DePree, *Leadership Is an Art* (New York: Doubleday, 2004), p. 11.

CHAPTER 9

I DIDN'T TAKE ENOUGH TIME TO THINK

*"Thinking is the hardest work there is, which is
probably the reason why so few engage in it."*
—Henry Ford

Oh, I spent plenty of time thinking, but my mental computer had downloaded the wrong software. When I went to Cornerstone, my clearest and most powerful desire was to build a church that would reflect well on the man God used to rescue me and turn my life around. I believed that, if Cornerstone didn't become bigger and better than Pastor George's church, Calvary, I would have failed to honor him. In every aspect of ministry, I hoped to add one good idea to everything he had taught me. Success, in my view, was easily measured by the number of people in our church and by their level of giving. Every molecule in me was energized to accomplish the goal of growing a bigger and better church.

How would this happen? I'm Pentecostal from my toes to what's left of my hair, but I quickly realized I don't have dramatic spiritual gifts. I admired anointed miracle workers like R. W. Schambach, A. A. Allen, Oral Roberts, and Benny Hinn, but people were not slain in the Spirit on a regular basis or miraculously healed on my platform. My box of dramatic works of God was empty. I'd seen plenty of dramatic evidence of God's power, but not by my hand or word.

On the other hand, Pastor George was a brilliant orator. He articulated his message crisply and beautifully; my diction was honed in prison, so it was, shall I say, a bit more casual. Pastor George turned a phrase better than anyone I've ever heard. Today, I could rattle off dozens of acronyms and phrases he used to package biblical concepts so people could remember them. When he taught about the variety of gifts and roles in the body of Christ, he told his people, "God didn't call you to be a carbon-copy-cookie-cutter Christian," and, "The genius of God is manifested in the diversity of God." At a funeral, he told the mourners, "Today, that dear saint breathes the rarified air of glory!" I don't know where he came up with so many memorable lines, but he used them in every message. It would take me a week to craft just one of them. I quickly realized his preaching gift was beyond me, too.

I had to do some soul searching: *I'm not as smart as Pastor George, and I'm not anointed like R. W. Schambach. What do I bring to the table that blesses people and expands the kingdom of God?* The answer was very clear: my hard work. Moses prayed, "Let the favor of the Lord our God be upon us; and confirm for us the work of our hands; yes, confirm the work of our hands" (Psalm 90:17). That's my prayer, too.

> *"Our soul needs time to think, dream and reflect."*
> —Jo Ann Davis

DRIVEN AND CONSUMED

During my first year at Cornerstone, I took only three days off. Two nights a week, I loaded and unloaded trucks to provide enough so our family could eat. On those days, I didn't sleep at all. In my first five years, our family didn't take a vacation. To keep my sermon preparation from interfering with all of my other responsibilities, I worked on my messages between 10:00 at night and 6:00 in the morning. I was working from early morning until pretty late at night … every day.

For five years, I worked like there was no tomorrow, until, one day, Pastor George told me bluntly, "Maury, you need to take a month off. You need the rest."

I answered in an instant. "I can't! I have too much to do."

Just as quickly (like he had anticipated my reaction), he said, "You've said I'm your spiritual authority, and the favor of God on your life is directly related to your submission to my authority. Is that right?"

"Uh … yes, sir."

He had boxed me in, and he knew it. He smiled. "Then you're going to take a month for a sabbatical, and you're going to take it with me."

My mind was racing. *I'll have to get approval from the board.*

Pastor George was prepared. He explained, "I've already talked to them, and they agree that you need a month off. It's approved." A couple of them had told Pastor George they were worried about me; they were sure I wouldn't last much longer if I didn't find a better rhythm for my life. They didn't say that to me, but they said it to him.

Pastor George's idea of a sabbatical wasn't to go to a monastery to study ancient manuscripts—which I'm sure is attractive to somebody. We went on a motorcycle tour around the borders and coasts of the continental United States. We saw some beautiful parts of the country.

> *"If you win the rat race, you're still a rat."*
> —Lily Tomlin

We had a ball, but I didn't learn very much. When we got back, I immediately returned to my rat-race lifestyle, except that, a couple of Fridays a month, I took road trips on my motorcycle. Sometimes, I rode to Gatlinburg; sometimes, I rode to Miss Patty's in Kentucky to have one of their incredible two-inches-thick pork chops. Sometimes, I rode to North Atlanta to eat at my favorite restaurant, Bahama Breeze—I love their conch chowder!

After a few of these trips, Sandy told me, "I hope you'll make your Friday motorcycle trips a regular part of your schedule."

I was surprised, and asked, "Why would you say that?"

"Because," she tilted her head and told me, "you're different when you get away for these trips … different in a good way."

On these one-day road trips, and even when our family began taking vacations, I called the church everyday (sometimes several times a day) to ask, "What's going on? Is there anything you need from me?" In fact, for the first 20 years as the pastor of Cornerstone, unless our family was on vacation, I took all emergency calls from 4:00 in the afternoon until 8:00 the next morning.

The Friday rides and family vacations were improvements, but they didn't affect my fundamental style of work. Probably the best word to describe that style is "immediate." If I had a question, I called the person right then. If I wanted to make a change, I made it without consulting anyone. I was on call for the church, and I expected everyone on our team to be on call for me. My leadership decisions were spontaneous, impulsive, impetuous, and often unnecessary. My thoughts were a tornado of minutiae; I didn't step back to consider the bigger questions that could really make a difference. I drove everybody crazy—including myself.

I'm not saying details aren't important, but I didn't have to know all the details all of the time, without delay. This is one of the facets of micromanaging. I believed I had to do all the thinking for everyone in the church, so I spent an incredible amount of time focused on matters that could have—and should have—been delegated. I should have trusted our people to manage their responsibilities with excellence.

I didn't leave the church on Sundays until I had an accurate count of people who had attended and the amount of the offering—to the penny. I couldn't wait, and I didn't look for trends. I lived service to service, day to day, moment to moment. My hyper-vigilance kept our staff team on edge. Some were anxious and fearful—they could get a demanding call at any time, day or night. Some were simply irritated that I asked about things they'd already told me. I often asked, "Tell me what you're doing right now. What's happening?" More than a few times, one of them told me, "Pastor, I already explained that I'd have this done by Thursday, and this is Tuesday. You're right. It's not finished yet, but it's not supposed to be. We're on schedule. We'll get it done." What they probably wanted to say but didn't was, "Leave me alone! Trust me to do what I said I'd do!"

My compulsive need for information was powered by my insecurity. I believed that more knowledge would protect me from failure. If I didn't know something, I was taking a risk of being hurt and looking foolish ... and I couldn't have that!

Through all these years, Gail was amazingly supportive. She appreciated the fact that I was working hard to build a great church to glorify God, so she gave me plenty of room. To be honest, I'm pretty sure that she didn't try to correct me because she knew I wasn't going to change. In that first year at Cornerstone, when I was working seven 15-hour days (except for the two 24-hour days) she wrote me a letter. I've always remembered one of the lines: "I can't wait until we're old enough that we're not working, and we can put our dentures in the same jar." That was her way of saying, "I really want to spend more time with you, but I realize that's not going to be anytime soon."

"I don't believe in burnout. A lot of people work really hard for decades and decades, like Winston Churchill and Albert Einstein.

Burnout is about resentment. It's about knowing what matters to you so much that if you don't get it, you're resentful."
—Marissa Mayer, CEO of Yahoo

STARTING TO THINK

People might ask, "Well, Maury, didn't you spend time thinking about all the work you were doing? And didn't you think while you were preparing your sermons?" My answer is that, for me at least, there's a world of difference between regulated thinking and unregulated thinking.

Let me explain: My mind never quit racing as I anticipated problems, found solutions, planned meetings, met with people, and prepared messages. My brain was running on 220 amps all day, every day, and my thoughts were always focused on the problem or opportunity at hand.

Unregulated thinking, in contrast, doesn't have an immediate agenda. After many years as a pastor, I began carving out an hour or two every week to sit with a couple of questions and a blank piece of paper. This was a time to dream ... to consider the *what ifs*. I might have a wide-open question like, *What can we do that will make our church more attractive to people in the community?* or *Do we really need this ministry or that one? Which ones are really making a difference, and which ones are draining our resources with very little impact?* or *What if we had our worship service at a different time of day?*

If I'd read a recent demographic study of the area, I'd ask myself, *How do we need to change to reach the people who now make up our community?* Or I might think about our family and consider, *What kind of vacation can we take next year that will give us more than a good time?*

This sounds healthy and beneficial, doesn't it? But for me, following through with this commitment was exceptionally hard. I tried everything: one hour, two hours, a full day, half a day, and two half-days. No matter what I tried, my default mode was to go back to the office and get back to the grind. I wanted to invest my time in things that would bring immediate and tangible benefits, and pondering the big issues didn't seem very effective.

Over the years, though, I've seen the payoffs of this kind of thinking time. A lot of pastors are like me—at least to some degree. The tyranny of the urgent crowds out the necessity of the important, and we keep running on the treadmill, faster and faster. When I consult with pastors about the importance of carving out time to think, I recommend starting small: put two one-hour blocks of time in the schedule every week. They can expand it to two two-hour times when they see the benefits—opportunities to ask questions that aren't on the top of the list during the rest of the week, but that can radically affect the emotional life of the pastor and the direction of the church.

> *To think is easy. To act is difficult. To act as*
> *one thinks is the most difficult of all.*
> —Goethe

If we try too much too soon, it's like the average person among us deciding to run a marathon next week: The results won't be good!

It's better to make a commitment to run (or run and walk) a mile for a week or two, and gradually add more distance as running becomes natural.

As I've seen the value of unregulated thinking, I've realized that I've always been an optimist, but I'm also an enthusiastic achiever without analytical thought. In other words, I'm driven to *do*, not to think. I took our board members to Colorado to do some planning, and we went hiking one day. When we got to a stream, one of the younger men looked at it and said, "I don't think I can jump across it." But I told him, "Watch me!" I took a flying leap and landed in the water several feet short of the rock I was aiming for. Man, that water was cold! That's just one of many, many illustrations of *doing* instead of thinking.

To be honest, I never really got this thinking thing right until I left my role as the pastor of Cornerstone. To help with our transition, I asked Sam Chand to advise us. He realized my propensity to stay involved, so he suggested a requirement that I not come to the office or call to get information from Galen or anyone else. Galen and I would meet on Thursdays so he could fill me in, but my compulsive micromanaging would have to stop ... not gradually fade—stop.

I've seen people go through withdrawal from drugs, and it's not a pretty sight. When they stop drinking alcohol, shooting up, or taking pills, their bodies often convulse with resistance to the change. When Sam drew that bright red line to keep me from being overly involved in the life of the church, I got a taste of what withdrawal must feel like. For a while, it felt terrible: awkward, confusing, and wrong. I didn't know what to do. I wanted to reach for the phone, but I had to stop myself from calling someone for information. After a while, though, I settled into a new normal. I read more books, took more trips, and relaxed much more.

In consulting with pastors around the country, I see more clearly the benefits of finding time to think. Recently, I met with a church's outgoing and incoming pastors to help them with their transition. We had long and productive conversations. At the end of the day, the exiting pastor gave me an invitation: "Maury, would you like to go out to dinner with my wife and me?"

I told him, "Thank you, but I need to go back to the hotel to think."

I'm not sure this is a sign of the End Times ... but it might be.

My unwillingness to take time to think was a result of an undercurrent of fear that I might not do enough to be a success. Our mission was godly, and our vision was right, but my actions were driven by anxious thoughts. Paul's letter to the Philippians is a thank-you note, because they had supported him in his missionary travels. Near the end of the letter, he acknowledges the damage caused by fear, and he gives them a remedy:

> Be anxious for nothing, but in everything by prayer and supplication with thanksgiving let your requests be made known to God. And the peace of God, which surpasses all comprehension, will guard your hearts and your minds in Christ Jesus. Finally, brethren, whatever is true, whatever is honorable, whatever is right, whatever is pure, whatever is lovely, whatever is of good repute, if there is any excellence and if anything worthy of praise, dwell on these things. The

> things you have learned and received and heard and
> seen in me, practice these things, and the God of peace
> will be with you. (Philippians 4:6-9)

A couple of chapters earlier, Paul included what was perhaps an early hymn sung in the churches. He described Jesus as the infinite Creator, the humble Servant, the perfect Sacrifice, and the exalted King (Philippians 2:5-11). I think this is where Paul wanted our thoughts to go when we're anxious, because Jesus is true, honorable, right, pure, lovely, respectable, excellent, and supremely worthy of praise. Fear and anxiety melt away when we think deeply about the love, power, and glory of Jesus. When we rivet our thoughts on Him, He gives us such peace that we can think more clearly about everything else in our lives.

People who are sold out to Jesus take action, but they aren't frantic or impulsive. When God's people were in exile and complaining that things weren't working out like they'd hoped, they blamed God for their problems. In Isaiah's beautiful affirmation of God's sovereignty and His covenant promise, he concludes with a word that applies to the people who are compulsive doers:

> He gives strength to the weary, And to him who lacks
> might He increases power. Though youths grow weary
> and tired, And vigorous young men stumble badly, Yet
> those who wait for the LORD Will gain new strength;
> They will mount up with wings like eagles, They will
> run and not get tired, They will walk and not become
> weary. (Isaiah 40:29-31)

Throughout my life, I don't think anyone would have said that one of my strengths has been patience or waiting. The ability to wait isn't just killing time; it's trusting that the God of the universe "gives strength to the weary," so we can relax and expect Him to do what only He can do. When we lead with this kind of confidence in God, we're role models for the people around us, God's Spirit is unleashed to do great things, and we don't drive ourselves crazy. That sounds pretty good to me.

Sandy Sterban volunteered to serve as a receptionist within six weeks of my coming to this small church called Cornerstone. As the church grew, so did she. She has served as a counselor, teacher, preacher in the pulpit, and sounding board for me personally through the years. She still serves in that capacity on occasion to my son, Galen.

I HAD THE PRIVILEGE OF working with Pastor Davis for 27 years as an associate pastor at Cornerstone Church. Longevity has given me the opportunity to observe him very carefully. He has many outstanding leadership gifts, but he was terribly impulsive in making decisions—little ones and consequential ones. For many years, he simply didn't take time to carefully consider the options—he just decided and let the chips fall. And they fell hard on many occasions.

When we had a position to fill on the team, he was willing to hire anyone with a pulse. He glanced at a resume, looked at the references, and noticed the quality of the person's connections. He gave them the job without making sure they could actually do the job or confirming what type of track record they had. I can't tell you how many times I told him he was making a big mistake by hiring someone who wasn't qualified. He sometimes pushed back; usually, he just shrugged and said, "Duly noted." But my warnings weren't duly noted at all. I told him, "Pastor, you're not listening!" Before long, he fired them and started the impulsive, unproductive process all over again.

Pastor Davis measured success by attendance, and he kept track of every person who was (and more particularly, wasn't) there on a Sunday morning. Every Life Group leader was assigned to call every person in their ministry each week to remind them to come to worship at Cornerstone. Then, the pastor over that ministry called the LG leader to make sure it was done. If someone missed two weeks in a row, he loudly complained that we weren't taking care of the sheep! It was our job to call them on Monday morning. Along with saying, "We missed you, and we hope to see you again soon," he wanted us to ask why they hadn't come and get a commitment for them to show up the next Sunday. Of course, we had to give him a report about our calls. Was it badgering? It was pretty close. It wasn't long before people saw our number on their caller IDs and refused to answer. A number of people left the church because they felt interrogated and pressured instead of loved.

From the first months of my time at the church, I had urged Pastor to get away and think about what God wanted him to do. I could see his exhaustion and weariness, so I'd beg him to take some time off. Finally, he took my advice. He'd get in his car or on his motorcycle and ride in the Smokies or the Blue Ridge Parkway. Sometimes, he'd ride down to Atlanta and back. He was always a different man when he got back. It was evident. His preaching was even more anointed, his anger was replaced with peace, he wasn't as erratic, he made better decisions, and his mood was tempered. It was like night and day. That's the reason I often pleaded with him, "Pastor, you're not thinking straight. Please get away!"

I'm not sure if this is true, but my guess is that his time in prison had a long-term effect on him. He probably felt easily closed in, and getting away on his motorcycle or in the car helped to clear his mind and restore his composure.

In spite of these idiosyncrasies, Pastor Davis was the best boss I ever had. He's the most complex and irritating human being I've ever known, but he is also the most generous, the most ethical with the church finances, and the most committed to excellence. He is a brilliant man, and he genuinely cares for people in the church and the community. Those traits may have been somewhat hidden when he was so driven and impulsive, but when he got away to think and pray, those qualities came shining through.

—*Sandy Sterban, Associate Pastor for*
Counseling, Cornerstone Church

MY ADVICE

I can certainly understand someone reading this chapter and saying, "He doesn't have the credibility in this area to give any advice." That's true, but at least I understand the problem, and I've taken at least a few steps in the right direction. Here's what I'm learning:

1) **Focus on the future.**

   We've all heard it a million times: "Leading is a marathon, not a sprint." We'll be much more fruitful over a longer period if we take the time to ask the big questions and spend plenty of time considering the answers.

2) **Create a healthy schedule that's sustainable and productive.**

   The cost of burnout is exceptionally high. Leaders who have little to no margin may look like godly, zealous warriors for God, but they often crash and burn. Many of the health problems suffered by church leaders are the direct result of exorbitant expectations, a demanding schedule, and the lack of a release valve. When we're too busy, too burdened, and too tired, we don't have the capacity to think clearly.

3) **Invite wise people to speak into your life—and listen to them.**

   If Pastor George hadn't been my spiritual authority, I'm quite sure I wouldn't have listened when he told me to take a month off. Over the years, other people tried to tell me the truth about my frantic lifestyle, but I wouldn't listen. Finally, I started listening to Sam Chand. It was late in my career—in fact, it hardly could have been any later—but God gave me ears to hear and a heart to respond to his good and godly advice.

Carving out time to think multiplies our creativity and provides fertile soil for fresh vision to take root and grow. When we introspect, God shows us areas that need our attention and reveals opportunities we didn't see before. Instead of having tunnel vision, we read, we pray, and we begin to see things from different perspectives. We can reflect on past conversations and gain insights we didn't have originally. When we're too busy, we don't take time to quiet our hearts to really listen to the Holy Spirit. A settled soul is responsive instead of reactive. *Reactions* are often defensive and destructive, but *responses* look for ways to understand, to connect on a deeper level, and to build bridges instead of destroying them.

CHAPTER 10

I STAYED STUCK IN OLD IDEAS

"Adaptability is the simple secret of survival."
—Jessica Hagedorn

For many years, I was so consumed with leading our church that I didn't pollenate my mind and heart with new ideas. I thought I didn't have time to go to conferences, and I didn't want to be away from our church to travel and see other churches. For a long time, the gas in my tank was what I learned from Pastor George. The concepts and principles I gained from my time with him took me a long way, but I didn't invest in refilling the tank.

When we introspect, we can identify the flaws that hold us back or that might cause us to forfeit the progress we've made. Relational interactions—the "iron sharpening iron" connections—stimulate our creativity, deepen our passions, expand our vision, and instill hope in us for a better future. We become like those we hang out with. If I spend a lot of time with golfers, I'll become interested in playing golf. If I hang out with civil engineers, I'll look at bridges a lot more closely. I started spending time with Ron McManus and Sam Chand, and their wit and wisdom began to rub off on me.

For almost my entire pastoral career, I spent time with a few men who were (and are) legends in our denomination. During these years, God was raising up a lot of dynamic young leaders, but I didn't rub shoulders with them—at least to any significant extent. These young leaders were experts in understanding the shifts in our culture, how to communicate the gospel to young people, and how to make disciples of young men and women in a world with many competing voices. They were learning, growing, and adapting so that they could be more effective; I was stuck in the past.

The reason so many ex-cons commit crimes again and go back to prison isn't that they love living in prison or because they hate freedom. The problem is that they didn't learn how to adapt to life outside the prison walls. They were still thinking, feeling, talking, and acting like they did when they were behind bars. The reason the ten spies reported to Moses that the people of God were too weak to take the Promised Land is that they were still thinking like helpless slaves. The reason 70 percent of lottery winners go broke within a few years isn't that they didn't win enough money. Instead, they didn't learn to think like people with wealth—so they spent money like there was no tomorrow. The welfare system was created to help people out of poverty, but it created a permanent underclass because it made people dependent on the government instead of encouraging them to build self-confidence and drive.

These are examples of people who settled for unexamined, unchallenged, institutional thinking. They had opportunities to acquire insights and to grow, but they didn't. For many years, I was like them: I didn't put myself in a place to think, feel, talk, and act differently than I did when I first became a pastor. I didn't learn, and I didn't grow. I got stuck.

NOT CHANGING WITH THE TIMES

If culture hadn't changed during the 80s, 90s, 00s, and 10s, being stuck in the past wouldn't have mattered much at all. But, as you may recall, there were a few changes during those decades! The personal computer, the Internet, and social media accelerated exponentially during this time. In fact, we now carry our personal computers in our pockets, and phone booths have gone the way of dinosaurs. Not that long ago, bi-racial marriages were rare; now, these relationships are common, and gay marriage is the law of the land. It wasn't too long ago that a law had to be passed to allow black people to vote; only decades later, we saw the election of the first African American president. Women have taken a more prominent role in business, government, and the church, the demographics of most communities has changed, and the Mamas and the Papas have been replaced by Jay-Z.

Where was I during all this? With my head down working like crazy to grow our church. I wasn't paying attention—and if the reality of a change surfaced, my reaction was to blast it instead of asking,

"What does this change mean to people who *need* Christ? What does it mean to people who *follow* Christ? How can I speak powerfully and graciously to this issue?"

We probably had the last choir in any church in America (maybe not, but it seemed that way). They sang beautifully, but people expected to sing along with what they heard on Christian radio stations. When we finally made a change to "modern music," we were still ten years behind other churches. You may have seen an old person wearing young, hip clothes. That's what our church looked like—we were trying hard to be cool, but we didn't make it.

In the worlds of business and the church, leaders have been moving toward collaborative teams. Writers like Patrick Lencioni, John Kotter, John Maxwell, and many others explain how to get the best out of people by empowering them and believing in them; I was still using a top-down, hierarchical, authoritarian management style. People right out of college who came onto our staff were very teachable and compliant, and they didn't seem to mind me telling them everything to think, say, or do; but when we hired people who'd been successful somewhere else and implied that our way was the only way—that everything they'd done before should be forgotten—we inadvertently sent them the message that we didn't value their experience and skills. I made all the decisions in their areas of ministry, and I kept track of all the details. They weren't growing because I wasn't letting them grow, and they knew it. They felt that I was taking them backward, and their motivation level plummeted.

Recently, Galen hired a marketing company to analyze Cornerstone's image in the Nashville area. After they conducted a thorough study, the company reported, "The reputation of your church is nothing like the reality of what we see here. Your dad was a hard-nosed, politically partisan, in-your-face, call-you-out and call-you-names-on-television kind of pastor. He attracted a certain profile of people … people who didn't mind being yelled at and being told they were messing up. But Galen, you're a loving, compassionate man, and the church is reaching out more than ever to care for people in the community. We need to do something about the church's public image."

Ouch.

Galen is much more caring than I am. When I see people standing on street corners holding signs and asking for handouts, I want to roll down the window and tell them, "Get a job!" I went on television and explained, "The Bible says, 'Let him who will not work not eat.' It's wrong … it's unbiblical for us to feed people who aren't willing to work to earn a living. We're harming them and disobeying God. Knock it off, Nashville!" (I'm not sure how our church got a reputation for lacking compassion!) Let me step back and say this: I truly believe the welfare system in our country is broken, and I'm convinced it often does more harm than good. But, I should have been much more measured in sharing my views.

There are, of course, those who are truly disadvantaged, and the Bible says that a sure sign of our hearts for God is the depth of our compassion for widows, orphans, the poor, immigrants, prisoners, the hungry, and the homeless. But we need to be wise in our generosity, giving people a hand up instead of merely a handout. I'll admit that I seldom made my case very attractively when I spoke, especially to those who are tenderhearted. My ill-advised method of communi-cating traditional American values caused a lot of needless damage to our church's reputation. Some of what I said was genuinely over-the-top, but much of it was true. Still, my communication was deeply flawed and hurtful to a lot of people.

I had every intention of building bridges to the African American community to tell them about Jesus and lead them to faith, but my antiquated thinking and my style of communication caused them to stay away in droves. I didn't sound like a loving, inclusive pastor who sees all races as created by God for His glory. Bridges and walls are both made from concrete, but the forms I poured it into made far too many walls that kept people out.

When our church was stuck in neutral in about 2010, I hired a company out of Dallas to do some research in our area and give us advice about how to start growing again. I was willing to do almost anything, as long as it honored God. A few weeks later, they presented their assessment: "Pastor, the average age of the people in your church has increased by five years in only the last four years. You aren't attracting many young families because the facilities for your chil-dren's ministry are out of date. Your worship center is very nice, but your facilities tell parents that their children aren't that important to you. They can find far better environments for their kids somewhere else, and that's the most important factor for many of them."

I swallowed hard, but they weren't finished. "You also have some children's staff members who are, we'll say, problematic." They didn't have to say another word. I had hired a guy to work in our children's ministry who was a retired mixed martial arts fighter. The kids loved him, but the parents were terrified when they saw him. I had hired another man who owned the largest tattoo parlor in Nashville. He was covered in very interesting skin art. Again, the kids were fascinated, but the parents weren't terribly impressed with my selection of personnel. Our church experienced "white flight" when very few black people were coming!

I thought I was progressive and ahead of the curve because I'd hired cutting-edge people who were rough around the edges but who had come to Christ and had fantastic testimonies; but that's the reasoning of tent revivals 50 years ago, not a church in a suburban, middle-class community.

> *"It is not the strongest of the species that survives, nor the most intelligent. It is the one that is most adaptable to change."*
> —Charles Darwin

I wish I could stop there in my list of boneheaded decisions, but there are more ... many more. I had an ironclad law that no kids under two years old were allowed in the sanctuary during any service. I made this rule crystal clear because I didn't want any baby's crying to interrupt worship. The consultant asked me, "Do you have any idea how many young couples left your church over this policy? Do you know how many walked out of services with babies in their arms *last Sunday* because an usher or greeter told them they had to put their child in the nursery?" This rule didn't hurt our church for about 20 years, but in the early 2000s, the culture shifted to be more accepting of children in every setting, including church services. I was still living in the past with my traditional, institutional thinking, and I missed the opportunity to attract and involve a lot of young families.

The cultural changes that took place in our society included some excesses, as all change does. Greater emphasis on raising healthy children also produced more than its fair share of "helicopter moms." I remember meeting a young mother after a service. She proudly told me her little boy was nine months old. I said, "He's cute. Why don't you put him down on the floor, so he can crawl around?"

She looked horrified and told me, "My baby has never been on a floor, and it won't start now!"

I wanted to say, "Well, I can fix that. Give him to me. I'll bounce him on the floor like a ping pong ball!" But for once, I didn't say what I was thinking. When I grew up, we played outside all the time. In the summer, we went barefoot. If we slid down a tree and got cut, we wiped the blood off and kept going. When our kids were young, they sometimes followed my example and rode their bikes without shoes on. Gail tried to get them to wear shoes, but I told her, "When one of them gets a toe caught in the spokes, he'll put his shoes on."

In 1976, Edward Hall used an iceberg as an analogy for culture. He reasoned that some aspects were visible above the water line, but the larger part was beneath the surface.[7] I only paid attention to the tip of the ice, when there was a whole world of information and behaviors underneath the surface that could have driven our success and informed my decisions.

---

7 "Edward T. Hall's Cultural Iceberg Model," *Beyond Culture*, 1996, https://www.spps.org/cms/lib/MN01910242/Centricity/Domain/125/iceberg_model_3.pdf.

CHANGE STARTS WITH ME

My rough background and my age conspired to keep me mired in the past. Actually, I don't want to blame anyone or anything for my intransigence. Other pastors studied the culture and found ways to communicate in meaningful ways as the times changed, but I didn't. The consultants who came to our church saw that my leadership wasn't going to work in the future. We had to change, but the church couldn't change until *I* was committed to change.

The startling revelation that Cornerstone was slowly dying was the spark that ignited a transformation in me. When I heard them use the word "death" several times, it got my attention. If I didn't get a better grasp of the contemporary culture, we were going to end up with a few blue-haired people whose goal for each day was finding their dentures.

I've applied a passage out of Hebrews to my need to be more observant of the shifts in our culture. The writer explained that Jesus was "according to the order of Melchizedek," both priest and king, but he chided the readers because they weren't studying and weren't perceptive of the application of truth. He told them they were still like infants, needing milk when they should be eating solid food. Then he wrote, "But solid food is for the mature, who because of practice have their senses trained to discern good and evil" (Hebrews 5:14).

When our senses are trained, we're sensitive, we're perceptive, and we can tell how the culture is changing, so we can shape our communication to be effective. Leaders need more than institutional thinking in modern times. Change is happening at an incredible pace. More than ever, we need to read authors who understand what's going on, we need to listen to podcasts by perceptive leaders, and we need to hang out with people who won't settle for things that worked in the past.

Ron McManus was a successful pastor in the Assemblies of God for a number of years before becoming a church growth consultant. I'd heard about Ron, but I really got to know him when I hired him in 2006 and as a consultant to Cornerstone Church. From 2006 to 2010, Ron helped us to move quickly from averaging 2,300 members to averaging 4,000. Over those years, he was another one of those people who became a friend for life.

⁂ • • • ⁂

ISOLATION IS ONE OF THE greatest problems pastors face in ministry. My name is Ron McManus, and I have known Maury Davis personally for about 20 years. One of my ministries is to consult with pastors and help do assessments of the local church.

Pastor Maury invited me to do an assessment of the ministry at Cornerstone Church. The church had grown rapidly over the years and was averaging around 2,500 in attendance. We worked together over several months to determine what was needed to reach the next level. As a result, the church grew over the next four years to over 4,000 in attendance. I've returned two more times over the years, and am presently working with Pastor Galen Davis as the church transitions to a new relationship paradigm.

Pastor Maury was a "command and control" leader and, like many megachurch pastors, a perfectionist by nature. Even when the church grew to several thousand, he continued to micromanage the ministry. The paid staff were given direction rather than the opportunity to be partners in the planning process. There was a lot of turnover in areas such as the children's ministry, youth ministry, and the executive pastor role. Because of his leadership ability, Pastor Maury was able to see the church grow, but he lived in isolation as a leader. Isolation gives you tunnel vision and makes you vulnerable to making bad decisions. Failure to process decisions with your team can cause you to be blindsided.

Pastor Maury had no problem making decisions, but many times after the fact, he would say to me, "I probably shouldn't have done that." The challenge for all strong leaders is learning to process decisions with a trusted mentor and your team before you do them. Over 50 percent of pastors live in isolation from other leaders in ministry. Our insecurities and lack of trust can keep a lid on our ministry and our church. For that reason, over 80 percent of churches are less than 200 in average attendance.

I've watched Pastor Maury grow in his desire to seek counsel from others. That is why I, as well as several other consultants, have worked with him over the years. One thing I know, also, is that he's lived with a great deal of pain because of his mistakes from 40 years ago as a felon. He's endured ridicule and horrible treatment from some media in Nashville regarding his past. He has a strong constitution—otherwise he would have left the ministry. Very few people know the pain he endured to build a great church in Nashville under the scrutiny of the media and politicians. I only wish he had opened up more, so that some of us—as friends—could have helped him. He lived with silent pain, in isolation, for many years. I remember one time when DDS in Nashville threatened to shut down the church daycare because Pastor Maury had been a felon. His crime had nothing to do with kids.

Today, Cornerstone Church is a great church because of the price paid by Pastor Maury. Under Pastor Galen's leadership, the church is recognized as the leader in Nashville, ministering to the needs of people.

—Ron McManus, Church Leadership Consultant,
Former pastor and Denominational executive

꒴ • • • ꒳

MY ADVICE

I've come very late to this party, but I'm here now. Maybe my struggle to relate to the new generations will provide some comfort, if not practical tools for growth.

1) **Connect with leaders outside your tribe and outside your generation.**

   If we "dance only with the ones who brung us," we'll remain backward in our thinking (like that line!), and we'll fail to connect with younger generations. If you're a young leader, you're probably already connected to your peers, so reach out to older people who have experience walking with God and wisdom you can glean. Their style of ministry may not be very hip, but they have treasured personal traits you value: integrity, passion, and tenacity.

When I realized that I hadn't cross-pollinated nearly enough, I asked Sam Chand, "Will you connect me with ten leaders anywhere in the world? I want to travel to visit them and learn all I can from them." I invited them to preach at Cornerstone, and I met with them to download everything they could teach me. Then, I traveled to their churches—from New Zealand to South Africa to every part of America—and saw how God was using them. They are some of the most amazing leaders in the world, and my horizons expanded. They taught me to see the church, individuals, and God in new ways.

I attended a service at Paul DeYoung's church in New Zealand and saw something I'd never imagined: the drummer had on ragged cutoff shorts and a tank top, and he had long, ratty hair. As the band played, thousands of people passionately worshiped God. Sam sat next to me. He leaned over and said, "You're having a hard time with this, aren't you?"

I whispered, "Sam, they don't even have a dress code!"

Paul overheard me and smiled, "Oh, yes, we do. No swimsuits."

You're probably thinking, "Man, Maury, you're so stiff you're going to break!" Exactly. I had to get away from the 20 acres of paradise known as Cornerstone Church to see how someone else thinks, prays, and leads a culturally relevant, incredibly effective church.

2) **Don't waste a crisis.**

Was it a crisis that our church had plateaued? Yes, absolutely. If an organization isn't growing, it'll start declining, and sooner or later, it'll lose any semblance of effectiveness. When that happened to Cornerstone, at first, I panicked. Then, I looked for help. I learned the most valuable lessons of my life only when desperation opened my heart to people who could teach me.

3) Be a student of the culture.

Subscribe to magazines or blogs that keep you informed about trends in the culture. You may not agree with everything you read, but you can be sure that many of the people who are listening to you agree with some of the things being said and written. As you become more perceptive about what's going on, your communication will be filled with wisdom and compassion, righteousness and justice. No matter what, *never stop learning*.

One of the primary roles of leaders is to tailor their message to a changing culture. If they don't keep their eyes open, they won't keep up with the change, and they'll become irrelevant.

I was confident the model of ministry that had worked in the past was the only one that could work in the present and the future. I was wrong. It took far too long for me to see the importance of knowing what needed to shift and what should remain unchanging.

EPILOGUE

SEVEN THINGS I DID RIGHT

I've been transparent in this book for one reason: to encourage other leaders to avoid the mistakes I've made. I'm not writing it to be sensational, and I'm not trying to do penance for my sin and shame. It is, though, one of the ways I'm apologizing to the people I've hurt over the years. I had the opportunity to gather many of them to express my sorrow. It brought, a number of them told me, a significant measure of God's healing … to them and to me.

Now, in the epilogue, I want to share some of the wonderful things God has done in my life and in our ministry at Cornerstone. Everything good is a testament to God's love, wisdom, and power. I've been honest about ten things I did wrong; I want to end with seven things that went right.

#1: I ANSWERED GOD'S CALL TO GO TO NASHVILLE TO BECOME THE PASTOR AT CORNERSTONE.

After serving at Calvary in Irving, Texas, I traveled as an evangelist for three years. In October of 1989, I was driving at night from

Tuscaloosa to Birmingham for the next revival. Gail and our three-year old triplets were asleep in the back of the van. Somewhere along the road, I saw a sign for the highway to Nashville. Suddenly, I sensed the Holy Spirit say, "I want you to go to Nashville and build a church." I'd never been to Nashville, and as far as I could remember, I didn't know anyone who lived in Nashville. It was, I quickly concluded, a crazy thought. But I responded, "Lord, if that's You, tell Gail."

A few minutes later, a voice from the back said, "Maury, have you ever thought about going to Nashville?"

I told her, "We're going tonight!"

"What?" She was incredulous.

"Go back to sleep," I said. "I'll wake you up when we get there."

A few hours later, as I drove over a hill and saw the skyline of Nashville, I wept. Instantly, the city became my heart's home, and it has never moved.

I planned to plant a church in Nashville, but the denomination asked me to take over a troubled church. It was Cornerstone. I believe that a clear sense of God's calling is essential for a fruitful ministry. When we go through the inevitable hard times, we need a bedrock of certainty to give us stability. Only in His will can we find His way.

I jumped in with both feet. Within 90 days, we'd painted the church, replaced the flooring, and weeded and replanted the flower-beds, and on Easter Sunday, people drove in to see a paved parking lot for the first time in the church's history. It was a glorious beginning … except when the youth pastor was arrested for theft, and we discovered he had been hiding a number of other sins.

The momentum God gave us in those early months carried us through the hard work of upgrading the facilities and overcoming a moral failure on our tiny staff team. A few months later, the church burned down and the fire department ruined our new parking lot when they drove their trucks on it. If I hadn't been sure I was called, I might have helped them put the fire out and then walked away. But I couldn't do that. I was doing exactly what God had called me to do, and I was doing it where He had clearly directed me.

#2: I HAD A BOLD, CLEAR VISION FOR THE CHURCH.

In February of 1990, Gail and I knew we were going to Nashville, but we hadn't moved yet. My parents had invited their kids and grandkids to have a winter vacation in Winter Park, Colorado. While other people were skiing and hanging out in the picturesque little town, I spent time praying. God gave me a promise from His Word: "'The latter glory of this house will be greater than the former,' says the LORD of hosts, 'and in this place I will give peace,' declares the LORD of hosts" (Haggai 2:9). I needed that encouragement. I'd been to Nashville to see the church, and, oh my—its glory needed a significant upgrade! Calvary in Irving had been my former glory, but God was saying that this little church would have even greater glory. To believe that, I needed His promise.

As I prayed, I asked God, "What kind of church do you want us to build?" The phrase came to mind: "We're a highly-disciplined congregation." This shaped my vision and my communication with our people. I often told them, "Cornerstone isn't just God's army.

It's His Green Berets, Navy SEALs, and DELTA Force!" Our people responded to this high calling, and they served with incredible passion and skill. No goal was too great to tackle, no obstacle too big to overcome. We were committed to being full gospel, completely committed to the Word of God, boldly evangelistic, and, for that day and time, progressive. The term has a different meaning in today's political climate, but for us, it meant that we were moving away from singing just hymns; we were adding contemporary music.

#3: I STAYED CONNECTED TO MY PASTOR.

Over the years, I've realized that my relationship with Pastor George was unique and rare. From the beginning, I saw him as my spiritual authority, and I can say without hesitation that everything good God has done in and through me has come because of him. I haven't made any significant decision without asking for his advice and blessing—and if he didn't bless it, I didn't do it.

A few years ago, I attended an "idea exchange" led by Karl Strader at Carpenter's Home Church in Lakeland, Florida. I had a new idea, and in fact, a plan. I talked to Pastor George to run the idea by him: "Pastor, I want to tell you something I'm thinking about doing, but I don't want you to give me your opinion for three days. During that time, I want you to pray about it. Can you do that?"

He said, "Certainly."

I wasn't convinced, so I insisted, "Pastor, I know you're going to want to respond immediately, so I want you to promise you'll wait three days."

He was getting frustrated with me. "Maury, I told you I'd wait three days."

I explained, "I think I need to do away with our Sunday night services."

He instantly reacted: "What? Davis, how much money do you pull in on Sunday nights?"

"Quite a lot."

"You can't do that! It's the dumbest idea I've ever heard!"

I waded back in. "Pastor, you said you'd withhold your opinion while you pray about it for three days."

He grimaced. "All right." But of course, he had already given me his opinion.

He didn't call me in three days, and he didn't call in three weeks. It was more than three months later that he called and said, "I think you need to give it a try."

Before I got the green light from him, I didn't talk to our board or our staff. There was no need to stir up the waters if I didn't have Pastor George's blessing. His blessings have changed everything about my life. When I had been out of prison for about a year, I was standing on the platform at Calvary before a service, and he asked me, "Davis, are you dating anybody?"

"No, sir," I answered.

"Why not?"

"Well, because you never give me any time off."

He continued, "If you were to date somebody, out of the hundreds of available young women in our church, who would it be?"

It didn't take long for me to formulate my response: "Pastor, I just got out of prison. These sweet church girls aren't going on a date with me. And besides, their daddies and mamas won't let them. I'm going to have to go to the red light district, lead one of those women to Christ, and then ask her for a date."

He knew I wasn't kidding. He was horrified. "You're not going down there!"

"Well," I answered, "I don't have any idea who would go out with me."

He scanned the stage and nodded toward the piano. "How about Gail Daniel?"

I shook my head. "Pastor, she's close to being engaged to a mortgage banker. How do you think an ex-con stacks up against him?"

He reached over, patted me on the chest, and said, "So?"

I took his action and his words as God's direction to marry Gail. A few days later, I called her boyfriend and asked him to go to the gym to work out with me. When we were finished and we were getting dressed, I told him, "I need to give you a heads up. I'm going to marry your girlfriend. I know y'all are pretty serious, but you need to know that I'm going to marry her."

I thought those might be fighting words, and I was ready, but he just shrugged, said, "Whatever," and walked to his car.

Two weeks later, a pastor called with an invitation to give my testimony at a tent revival in a little town south of Dallas the next Friday night. I said, "I'd love to."

He called back about an hour later to ask, "Do you know anybody who plays the piano?"

"I might," I answered with a grin. "Let me see if she's available."

I called Gail to ask her if she'd be interested, and she instantly responded, "I'd love to!" Her grandfather was the pastor of a pioneer church in Arkansas, so she had tent revivals in her blood.

I told her, "You can invite your boyfriend if you want to."

That Friday, we met in the church parking lot so the pastor who invited us could pick us up and drive to the revival. I asked Gail, "Where's your boyfriend?"

"Oh," she rolled her eyes. "He said he had to stay home and walk his mother's dog. He lives with his parents, in case you didn't know."

I thought, *Oh man, this is going to be a lot easier than I thought! He's a mama's boy!*

I gave my testimony and she played that night. When the pastor brought us back to Calvary, it was about 9:00 PM. I'd never had a conversation with Gail that was more than a few words here and there. I asked, "Would you like to go somewhere to get something to eat?"

She replied, "Yes, I'm starving!"

She got in my car, and we drove off. I'm pretty sure she expected me to take her to a diner or some other greasy spoon, but I took her to the nicest Greek restaurant in the area. I ordered dishes for two, the band was playing softly, and we sat together in the candlelight. I was really working on her. When we got up to leave, she had a pained expression on her face. She told me, "I feel like I'm cheating on my boyfriend."

"Don't worry about that," I assured her. "I already told him I'm going to marry you."

She was understandably shocked.

About a week later, I was preparing to give the message at a funeral when Gail walked in. She asked, "Are you preaching?"

"Yes. Are you playing?"

She nodded. I asked her, "You know, it's not a coincidence. How many more people does God need to kill for you to agree to marry me?"

I was just getting started. I went by to see her. I took flowers to all the ladies in her office with notes asking them to help me win her heart. They became my allies. One day, I went by her apartment early in the morning and let the air out of her tires and then offered to take her to work. I got them filled up later in the day so she'd appreciate how helpful and attentive I was. I basically ran Gail down until she agreed to marry me.

Would I have married Gail if Pastor George hadn't prompted me? I doubt it. Would I have married a prostitute? Probably not, but there's no way to know what course my family life might have taken. Everything good and right in my life—my salvation, the roles I've had in churches, my wife, my children, and the growth of Cornerstone—are because of Pastor George's influence.

#4: MY PASSION FOR JESUS AND FOR PEOPLE HAS NEVER WAVERED.

I hear people talk about backsliding, but that hasn't happened to me. I'm pretty sure my salvation story is the reason I haven't stumbled. If God would reach down into the bleakness of prison to rescue a man who had committed the most heinous crime, how could I ever turn my back on Him? To other people, His grace may not be as big of a deal, because they're not aware of how lost they were before they trusted in Jesus; to me, it's absolutely amazing.

I've always had a heart for people. At Cornerstone, we've always taken care of our people. Every day, we visit those who are in the hospital. If you lose a mother, father, brother, sister, son, daughter, or spouse, one of us will be at the funeral—no matter where it is or how far we need to travel. For the first ten years, that person was me, unless it was a Sunday. We don't call to ask if the bereaved church member wants us to come—we just come. The person might have been in a car wreck, in the hospital, or in jail; when we find out about the need, we show up. We put our arms around those who are hurting and communicate our love and care. I think we've had a higher level of pastoral care than any church I've ever heard about.

Praying with people over the phone isn't good enough. We show up; we don't use the excuse, "Well, people who are grieving want to be alone." They might feel alone, but that's why we go. I've never visited anyone who's lost a loved one who has told me, "I wish you'd go away." Instead, I've had countless people tell me, "I didn't know how much I needed you to come see me. Thank you, Pastor."

#5: I PUT THE KINGDOM OF GOD FIRST.

In my decisions, the primary filter isn't what's comfortable, what makes people happy, or what makes me look good. God gives bountiful blessings, but when Jesus said, "Follow Me," He meant for us to follow Him in sacrifice and obedience, no matter how inconvenient or painful it may be. My pleasure, my comfort, my reputation, and my agenda are secondary at best. Jesus challenged us, "If anyone comes to

Me, and does not hate his own father and mother and wife and children and brothers and sisters, yes, and even his own life, he cannot be My disciple" (Luke 14:26). In this passage, He's not advocating that we despise the people closest to us in order to prove our loyalty. Instead, he's using the term "hate" as a contrast. In comparison to our love and devotion to Jesus, our love and devotion to those in our family should be far, far less. We still love them, but not as much as we love Jesus. We're still loyal to them, but nowhere as close as to our loyalty to Him.

This means that, when our family has been on vacation and someone in the church needs me, I leave to be with that person. Idolatry is putting anyone or anything in God's rightful place in our lives, including our affections and our choices. He deserves to dictate our decisions. That's a kingdom perspective. I've heard some pastors insist, "We should always put our families first." I don't mean to be rude, but if they're first, Jesus can't be. This commitment doesn't mean we neglect our spouse and kids—just the opposite. When they see us put God's kingdom first, it challenges the selfishness in every human heart, and we're a model for them to follow. When we love Jesus well, we'll love our families well. But if we love them first, we'll smother them with attention and direction, making them feel incompetent to make their own decisions, and they'll perpetuate this misplaced devotion in the next generation. That's not the legacy I want to leave behind.

When we were much younger, some who watched how Gail and I parented our kids warned, "You're going to lose your kids." We didn't lose them—we took them with us to almost everything we did. They weren't neglected. They became partners in our work for the kingdom.

They learned that ministry is who we are and what we do as a family. Life isn't about our pleasure, our prestige, our comfort, or our control; life is about pleasing God by being humble, obedient children who delight in His love and give everything we've got to the greatest enterprise the world has ever known: fulfilling the Great Commission.

Someone asked Galen why people in our family talk about church all the time. He responded, "I'm not sure what you mean. Why are you asking?"

The person said, "It just seems that you have only one topic of conversation. You always talk about the church."

He responded, "It's the only thing that matters."

#6: WE CREATED FACILITIES FOR THE NEXT GENERATION.

A few years ago, I realized that my rigid, ingrown, institutional thinking had led me to create buildings that were decidedly old-school. Our previous sanctuary had little room in the lobby for people to gather and talk. The loud-and-clear message was this: "It's not important for you to get to know each other. What really matters is inside the sanctuary. Come in here, worship, hear God's Word, and I'll tell you everything you need to know!" Our new facilities speak a different message: "Getting to know each other is vitally important. Enjoy conversations, meet new people, and look at the waterfall." Our baptistery was moved from the platform to the common area so people can gather around and be close in that sacred event. Our children's facilities are no longer a disgrace. We now have three beautiful main rooms with state-of-the-art technology. In fact, our children's ministry building cost more than our sanctuary—that's a clear statement of what we value. We built a fireplace for the room where our senior adults meet. Every ministry has a brand new or newly-decorated building, and all of them say, "Let's do life together!"

We've finally caught up with the culture, and Galen is committed to staying ahead of the curve by anticipating the kind of facilities the church will need in the future. It took me decades to get beyond institutional thinking. He's already there.

#7: I'VE LEARNED FROM GIFTED COACHES, CONSULTANTS, AND COUNSELORS.

I've seen the necessity of having "outside eyes" look at what we're doing and give honest feedback. The role of a pastor has internal conflict between bold vision and tender compassion. Most of us drift toward one or the other, and we need someone who understands this tension to tell us when we're leaning too far one way.

Experts aren't as affected by the complexity of personal relationships and the history of painful or wonderful experiences on the team, so they can give objective input. I see pastors as riverboat captains: We're steering the boat around islands and snags in the water, all while trying to help the people on the boat learn their roles. It's easy for our attention to leave the water, and we can run aground on a barely submerged sandbar. A consultant reinforces what we're doing well and points out areas of need. Quite often, our minds can be consumed by one particular problem, and we're so distracted that the organization suffers. A person from the outside can help us compartmentalize the problem and find a workable solution so that it no longer dominates every waking hour.

Very few pastors have invited an expert to step in to help them. I'm quite aware that many can't afford a paid consultant, but everyone can find a wise, experienced pastor to serve as a mentor. A mentor will need to work a pastor into his or her schedule, but that's far better than flying blind. What I'm saying is that having "outside eyes" is absolutely crucial, and there's no excuse for not having someone play that role.

My life and my leadership are different because of the impact of Ron McManus and Sam Chand. Ron saw my top-down leadership style (How could he have missed it?) and showed me the value of collaborative leadership. It revolutionized how I led our team, and now, how I help the pastors who have asked me for assistance. Ron's influence helped us grow from 2,500 to 4,000 in a little over three years; when he left, I took our church back down to 3,400. Sam has focused on my thinking process. Under him, I've learned to challenge my assumptions and be honest enough to admit when I've been wrong. I'm a better leader and a better person because of him.

BEFORE WE GO

I love sports, and I enjoy finding out what factors contribute to a person winning or losing. The most accomplished athletes may not have more raw talent than another competitor, but they get the most out of their ability by training, preparing, and doing whatever it takes to excel. For much of my life as a pastor, I didn't invest enough in learning and training. Yes, God worked powerfully, but our church was held back by my false assumptions and mistakes as a leader.

Sports stories of gifted athletes failing because of a lack of preparation are sad and tragic, because they show us examples of those who didn't put in the work to maximize their God-given talents. For athletes and pastors, living with "what ifs" is a terrible way to end a career. I've shared my "what ifs" with you so that you can identify yours and do whatever it takes to eliminate them.

When I'm done, I want to pass a baton—not a cane.

ABOUT THE AUTHOR

After a troubled childhood and eight-and-a-half-years in prison, Maury Davis embraced his calling to spend his life and energy in full-time ministry. The opportunity to start at the bottom as a custodian in a megachurch led to his promotion to Youth Pastor. After his marriage to Gail Daniels and the birth of triplets, he launched into full-time evangelism with a focus on young people. He had many opportunities to go into the schools of our nation and present a life-changing message to students from every segment of society. On the first Sunday of February 1991, Maury preached his first sermon to the 250-member Cornerstone Church, where he went on to serve as Senior Pastor for over 27 years. The congregation grew to a maximum attendance of 4,000 in 2010.

Cornerstone planted eight other congregations in America that now have a combined attendance of almost 15,000 people every weekend. Cornerstone's international outreach included building, resourcing, and helping to plant 2,000 congregations in a 10-year period in Kenya.

Maury Davis's unique ministry allowed him to launch and experience a miraculous growth on the Nashville local CBS affiliate that became Middle Tennessee's number one viewed Christian broadcast on local or religious channels. He has been found on major networks and programming such as Praise the Lord with TBN, Daystar with Marcus Lamb, Fox News with Governor Mike Huckabee, as well as producing for TBN Africa a program that covered the African continent and Western Europe.

His passion for missions and love for people have taken him to Russia, Thailand, Cambodia, Singapore, Sri Lanka, Hong Kong, Manila, Panama, Barranquilla, Colombia, South Africa, Kenya, Nigeria, Tanzania, Swaziland, and India—he even had the opportunity to join Joyce Meyer in Africa for one of her major crusades.

Maury's rare perspective on leadership development and church growth, combined with his relationships with people, have created a global presence. In this season of life, with his unique experiences, he is focused on coaching and consulting the next generation of leaders and entrepreneurs to achieve their dreams and goals.

Maury resides in Nashville, Tennessee, with his wife and four children and their spouses, and six grandchildren.

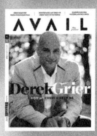

AVAIL LEADERSHIP PODCAST

WITH VIRGIL SIERRA